APOCALYPSE:

A Blessing in Disguise

by

Brother Alexius Dougherty, F.S.C.

ACW Press
5501 N. 7th Ave. #502
Phoenix, AZ 85013

Printed in the United States of America

ISBN 1-892525-23-2

ACKNOWLEDGEMENTS

May I single out the Most Rev. G. Patrick Ziemann in gratitude for the spontaneous goodwill and resourceful zeal his seven years' ministry has impacted upon our sprawling northern California Diocese of Santa Rosa. We who are consecrated Religious are especially mindful of his charaismatic talent for interlocking, so to speak, a lively *esprit de corps* amongst so many diversified apostolates.

I am further indebted to Bishop Ziemann for reviewing this treatise. His gracious comments were an affirmation that I was being scholarly, comprehensive, and on the right track with regard to apocalyptic symbolism.

TABLE OF CONTENTS

INTRODUCTION

Apocalypse: A Blessing In Disguise, not only touches on our Lord's redemptive role in salvation history, but on the "woman's" apocalyptic presence as well (Apoc 12:1). While it is true that the "woman" has eschatological reference to the Church, the Mystical Body of Christ would be incomplete without Our Lady's vital presence and vice versa. The reasoning for this is that Adam, shameful for having deprived all posterity the immediate benefits of earthly paradise, was divinely promised the messianic restoration of humanity through the merits of a Second Adam born of his seed. As for Eve, her personal shame came in the Garden of Eden for having betrayed her supportive role as Adam's helpmate. But she too was heartened by the divine revelation that the serpent's head would be crushed for all time under the foot of one of her female descendants (e.g., the second Eve, Mary, Mother of the Church).

How is it then that apocalypse is a "blessing in disguise"? Because as a divine revelation it is prophetically tailored to alert our fallible human condition in the area of moral decision making. The non-angelic Adam, for example, left unaided by God's providential care would be quite vulnerable to deception. And, although he was not alerted to a specific deceiver, his whole physical, intellectual and spiritual capacity had need of being fearfully and lovingly bolstered to circumvent the slightest diabolical hint of deception vis-a-vis God's edict in the Garden of Eden. First of all, this safeguard was divinely extended to him through God' s friendship with him. Secondly, God's edict alone was enough to focus Adam's awareness on the will of God; on his own free will; on his own freedom of choice; on the goodness of God's will that he make the right moral decision set before him. As for the open question of Adam making the wrong decision, God's edict alone was enough to give him an ominous awareness of some potential dark gulf between his freedom of choice and *God's* will. Unknown to him, such an apocalyptic gulf could be nothing less than the guilt of original sin—a kind of universal cause of damnation.

Little did he know about the particulars of his intercessory calling to his posterity. And so, we get our first clue to the enlightening grace of apocalypse, or divine revelation assisting his free will. That Adam could be forewarned even by the barest notion of the existence of evil was no small spiritual awakening. It was, so to speak, his Book of Revelation. That he might use that inner light advantageously to firm up his resolve to obey God's edict was a blessing in disguise. In the overall picture, apocalypse relegates both prospects of good and evil into the category of conditional prophecy. It is in that manner that God's edict justly felicitated Adam's freedom of choice and stirred up his instinctive capacity as a rational animal.

In his test of obedience, therefore, the bone of contention was his intermediary mission to posterity. For, as a direct and unconditional prerogative of grace, his obedience was a sinless means to an end. And, as such, it would nullify any alternate punitive providential means of universal spiritual restoration in Christ. Hence, it happened that our earthly paradise was squandered (apocalyptically incinerated, if you will) by the sin of our first parents. For, although mankind's fate was immediately promised messianic restoration, it would occur at the punitive cost of original sin with all its painful consequences. And so, we begin to expand the definition of apocalypse. Above all, apocalypse has no literal reference to a cataclysmic ending (see below) of our physical world. The intent of apocalyptic language focuses on the apocalyptic ending of a *spiritual* world. In this case, earthly paradise.

As a direct result of Adam's disobedience his compromised intermediary prerogative of grace to mankind was mercifully transferred into a second apocalyptic scenario. That is to say, God's attention shifted towards His beloved chosen people and anointed theocracy, the House of Israel. Briefly, the House of Israel's mosaic test of faith through, with and in Christ's anticipated redemptive act of obedience to his Father's will was also an intermediary prerogative of grace. As such, Israel's mosaic calling was a meritorious means to mankind's direct and unconditional messianic restoration. The significance of this is that Israel's messianic entrance (at the tireless behest of Jesus of Nazareth) into the Church's gospel mission to mankind would not require for them yet a third intermediary (gospel) testing of faith. On the contrary, Israel's sufficiently applied mosaic test of faith would have merited a direct and unconditional right to Christ's gospel mission of universal restoration (Church unity). In effect, Israel's mosaic test of faith had the potential of meriting mankind's universal restoration in Christ by being thoroughly endowed charismatically with the gifts of the Holy Spirit. It follows from this, of course, that a faithful Israel would not have nailed Christ to a cross. Nor need he have suffered complete oblation to satisfy his Father's will. One drop of his blood shed in union with his Father's will was of infinite value, "for the redemption of many".

Sadly, just as happened to our disobedient first parents, the unfaithful House of Israel was given an alternate means of grace, punitive in nature and providentially assured of messianic incorporation. Thus, although it had been promised messianic unification by virtue of God's covenant with Abraham, it contemptuously ignored the prophetic voices crying out to it from the bowels of its people's turbulent history. Its sin of omission was in suppressing the inspired mixed signals of conditional prophecies, or types divinely designed on the one hand to encourage faithfulness, and on the other hand, painted ominously in cataclysmic language as portents of the wages of sin and apostasy. What better Book of Revelation for all ages of Israel's sacred promised land to scrutinize and ponder than the two related conditional prophesies, namely, the glorious repentance and conversion of the Ninevites at the preaching of Jonah in contrast to the ominous experience of Jonah in the whales belly (Christ's conditionally prophesied rejection by his chosen people)?

Within the dimensions of this definition of apocalypse two reasons might be deduced as an explanation of Christ's "end of the world" theme which he employed to describe the House of Israel's insufficient response to his gospel message. Up until the Synagogue had officially rejected him he had always tenaciously held out hope for its conversion. His subsequent bitter tears over the city of Jerusalem attests to that. Those tears, of course, would have been pointless if the ancient prophecies often quoted by him regarding Israel's mosaic compromise had not been conditional prophecies. But Israel's point of no return came relatively early during his public life when the Temple officially met to plot his death. The high priest's rending of garments left a void in his human heart—-a void that only the cataclysmic language of eschatologic chaos could adequately describe. At that precise moment the House of Israel's direct and unconditional mosaic invitation (as chicks to the mother hen's wings) vanished, so to speak, in a fiery inferno.

Coincidentally, an even more impelling need had to be addressed by Christ as he surveyed the House of Israel's doleful eschatologic woes. It concerned the needs of the Church he was soon to found on the rock, Peter. It concerned the welfare of his mystical body, destined to become salvation history's third and final intermediary agency of grace for fulfilling God the Father's will of universal faith and incorporation of all mankind through, with and in the providential agency of His Son's infinite redemptive merits. It too was to be an intermediary prerogative of grace vulnerable to the sin of omission. In testimony of this we have but to review the traditional Church's all too frequent periods of gross laxity, renewed to fervor just as frequently through the miracle performing examples of saintly traditional Church reformers. Put in another way, at the "acceptable time" known only by God, the traditional Church's gospel legacy would determine its Christ-like image through which its gospel mission to mankind would be accountable.

The onus was on the traditional Church, therefore, to maintain a spiritual continuity in conformity with its gospel prerogative of directly and unconditionally influencing mankind's spiritual attraction to Christ. To help the Church sufficiently keep those traditional values viable, therefore (by way of directing its attention to the diabolical range of sin along with its hideous consequences), Christ laid the foundation of The Book of Revelation by his scathing "end of the world" theme which predicted the Temple's apocalyptic fate. Obviously, the nature of the Church's gospel mission as inherited by the Gentiles was beyond the apocalyptic scope of Old Testament prophets, for that would have decided Israel's fate. Hence, Jesus Christ, the greatest of all prophets was the only prophetic source the Church had upon which to establish an inspired biblical status for the Book of Revelation.

In stark contrast to this definition of apocalypse—tailored as it is to fallible mankind's free will by way of conditional prophecy—we see that Lucifer's fall from heaven was not apocalyptic. As an angel of light he was beyond the need for enticements and precautionary safeguards of conditional prophecy. His *non serviam* was enough to seal his fate eternally. Paradise remained intact while he was unceremoniously trumpeted into Hades. And other hosts of angels who willingly joined his forces shared the same fate.

My interpretation of the Book of Revelation is an attempt to display Mary's apocalyptic role, and is meant to be taken in an accommodated sense. Its purpose is to search out "signs of the times", so topical during today's growing symptoms of millennial fever.

If we can visualize the timing of Mary's Fatima apparitions as providentially critical to the condition of the Church's Christian image (or 2000 years' gospel legacy), then her urgent requests for Church reform take on an

added eschatological meaning. For example, her two stipulations for "peace" are significant. Her first "if" clause regarding the Church's long overdue need for thorough reform guaranteed unconditional peace to the world: "If my
requests are granted, Russia will be converted and there
will be peace." But, had not Mary added yet another "if"
clause to her stipulation for peace, one that guaranteed
only a qualified period of peace, we would never have
guessed the eschatological significance she was giving to
"Russia," or to "Russia's conversion," or to "peace".

Why was Mary's message of peace qualified then, except in the context of the Book of Revelation's conditionally prophesied eschatological interruption of Church
unification as expressed by the "unchaining" of Satan? "If
my requests are not granted, Russia will spread its errors
throughout the world raising up wars and persecutions
against the Church. Many will be decimated. In the end,
my Immaculate Heart will triumph and a *period of peace*
will be given to mankind."

To sum up, therefore, the Fatima generation's insufficient response to the Church's last chance for acquiring
world peace (Christian unification in Christ) through traditional reform, shackled the Church's mission with an
alternate providentially permitted punitive agency of grace,
namely, the world's reduction to a near condition of moral
futility in the wake of Soviet Russia's rape of mankind.
Unfortunately for the Church, such a punitively gained
crisis—motivated conversion of mankind is also strapped
with an eschatological proviso, that only the speedy appearance (*parousia*) of a triumphant Christ's second coming will be able to remedy.

What that very favored Fatima generation (1917—

1967) failed to realize, therefore, was that traditional Church reform of itself weighed in the balance at Fatima. Up to that time it had been Catholicism's only available spiritual means for renewal throughout the centuries by which it could maintain the Church's Gospel prerogative. In other words, if traditional Church reform went by the wayside, so too would disappear Catholicism's Gospel prerogative for attaining Satan's direct and unconditional defeat. This can only lead to the conclusion that Mary's apparitions at Fatima addressed the Church at the "acceptable time" of Gospel accountability for its mustard seed calling over Satan in salvation history. At that historic moment a whole Catholic generation (the Fatima generation) was made accountable for the Church's 2000 years' Gospel legacy. The Church was exhorted to respond- —at least to a sufficient degree-—to Mary' s urgent last chance invitation for utilizing its intermediary Gospel advantage over Satan's "mystery of iniquity". In short Catholicism's sufficient response to the Fatima message of peace would have obviated the opening of Vatican II (as the Church's entrance point into mankind's final days of unification in Christ). Taken in this sense, Mary's pivotal hortative role to the Church paralleled Our Lord's hortative role to "his Father's house", during Israel's Messianic "acceptable time".

Hence, the Church' s traditional reform movement is not an issue here—as though it should be maintained at the expense of Vatican II. The intriguing quality of Vatican II is that it providentially adjusts the Church's mission to mankind by adapting it to the changing times. But this, at the same time, is its weakness. The subtlety here is that it isn't the Church that should have changed for the times—

it is the times that should have changed commensurately with a growing church. Once Catholicism's insufficient growth-rate allowed the times to get out of hand, it became providentially expedient for the Church to mitigate "the more excellent way" St. Paul spoke of.. .by a temporary double standard, if you will. For example, Moses began handing out bills of divorce, but only as a gentler providential remedy for his people's hardness of heart. The culprit, therefore, is not Vatican II, as arch-conservatives would have us to believe. In retrospect, Vatican II reforms have successfully addressed some of the areas responsible for the real culprit, pre-Vatican II's insufficiently formed Christian image.

And so it happened that three Portuguese children echoed the traditional requirements of Church reform in the simple language of youngsters: "Do penance, avoid doing bad things, pray the rosary, etc." The question arises, however, what impact would their simple witness have had upon their society without an assist from "the Miracle of the Sun?" The prodigious signs and wonders performed by Jesus himself answer this question by the precedent he set for church reform: "Otherwise believe for the very works' sake" (John 14:12). We have but to recall with nostalgia the venerable names and works of saintly church reformers and founders of religious orders to realize what an enormous supernatural tradition has quietly dried up within our Church's apostolic cause since the opening of Vatican II.

PART ONE

*The Apocalypse
Unveiled*

I

AN APOCALYPTIC SENSE

The death and resurrection of Jesus Christ is the all embracing theme of Holy Scripture. "Then he said to them O foolish, and slow of heart to believe in all things which the prophets have spoken. Ought not Christ to have suffered these things, and so to enter into his glory" (Luke 24:25-26)? And yet, although Christ's death is the focal point of sinful mankind's relationship with God, it was not the divine starting point of God's relationship with man. We must keep in mind Adam's freedom of choice in the Garden of Eden also presupposed a providential scenario that obviated the necessity of Christ's complete oblation.

What we are saying here is that even if Adam required the anticipated grace of the Son of man's obedience in order to cooperate meritoriously with God's edict in the Garden of Eden, this prevenient grace did not nor could not originate from the death of our divine Savior. And for two reasons. First, Adam did not have need of the grace of redemption before he sinned.

Secondly, St. Augustine was not being accurate when he designated Adam's sin of disobedience as a "happy fault that brought us such a Redeemer." In reality, Adam's sin of disobedience could not of itself bring to us the crucified Christ. For that would dictate that the divine redemptive remedy for Adam's sin required yet another sin (i.e. deicide) to be committed before he and all future mankind could be redeemed. Such a precondition as that is contrary to the ways of divine grace. How, then resolve this difficulty? For this we need an Apocalyptic sense.

First Apocalypse

By studying the circumstances of the fall of Adam, as well as the strikingly similar circumstances surrounding Israel's apostasy, we begin to perceive yet another mysterious influence intertwining man's salvation history, namely, apocalypse. First of all, these two correlated falls from grace reveal three identical providential aspects: mission, prerogative and promise. It is extremely important to note that, as in the case of Adam's test, the House of Israel's freedom of choice likewise presupposed a providential scenario that obviated the necessity of the Incarnate Word's extreme redemptive remedy of obedience unto death. Holy Scripture never indicated that the Son of man was sent by his Father to die on a cross. He came simply to do his Father's will.

Adam's apocalyptic ending of paradise, therefore, brought fallen mankind a promised Redeemer—but not a crucified Redeemer. Rather, Adam's fall engendered a second calling and apocalyptic format tendered by God in view of a promised Messiah to Abraham's Israel, His chosen theocracy. For us to appreciate, therefore, the overall scope of Israel's providential calling into the New Jerusalem, in through, and by the anticipated merits of the obedient Word made flesh, we must bear in mind the apocalyptic circumstances involving Israel's test of faith. Obviously, any Old Testament scriptural revelations (apocalypses) of final dire consequences to the House of Israel would have to be conditional prophecies in order to safeguard Israel's test of faith and freedom of choice. Hence, through the centuries the House of Israel maintained the efficacious inspiration (conditional prophecy) of Nineveh's penance right up to the day of her official rejection of Christ. As a result, Israel's apocalyptic exclusion from the New Jerusalem's (the Church's) gospel mission to mankind was just as devastating to her as was Adam's apocalyptic exclusion from paradise.

In short, Israel's Mosaic prerogative would have entered herself and all mankind directly and unconditionally into the embrace of her divinely promised Messiah and fellow countryman, Jesus of Nazareth, of whom the shedding of one drop of blood in obedience to his Father's will would have been sufficient to defeat the works of Satan through the completion of his Mystical Body, the Church. To repeat, even though Israel's pathway to the Messiah was divinely promised, her apocalyptic exclusion from the Church's direct and unconditional gospel mission for reconciling mankind with one another in Christ was just as punitive and devastating to her as was Adam's apocalyptic exclusion from the Garden of Eden—where he had once "conversed openly with God."

Mission, prerogative, promise. How does Apocalypse enter Adam's picture? Surely not in the divine promise given by God to Adam of a coming Messiah springing from his very seed. Paradoxically, Apocalypse would be impossible without that promise. The reason is that Apocalypse, strictly speaking, is a human scenario...a scenario in need of divine Mercy. Poor Adam, dust of the earth, could be swayed both by the double talk of a serpent and the sweet talk of a woman. In view of these human limitations, his test was prefaced by the divine revelation that his idyllic

world of paradise could continue unabated, or suffer a pro-
hibitive change. Only to the tested human spirit does God
employ the use of apocalypse. By it He arouses man's instincts as surely as He inspires their hearts and minds with
love and understanding.

Thus, His veiled warning to Adam is the first element
essential to the definition of Apocalypse that we deduce
from the biblical story of Adam's test in the Garden of
Eden. When we reflect on how directly God dealt (without promises or warnings) with His rebellious angels, we
see the unique human situation Adam was in. As a pure
spirit, Lucifer's intellectual act of pride was an unpardon-
able sin against the Holy Ghost. His allegiance to God of
itself was an ultimatum, and not subject to divine promises or threats. It is just and merciful, therefore, that Adam's
apocalyptic (Paradise-ending) "happy fault" was not pun-
ishable by the same eternal rejection meted out to Lucifer's
non serviam.

It is true that an omniscient God foreknew Adam's
fall even before the test was tendered. On the other hand,
only God could reveal the reward due to Adam for his
faithful obedience. Hence, He safeguarded Adam's free
will and peace of mind by revealing not his destiny (which
would have devastated Adam), but his conditional status
(reward or punishment). As a result, Adam's destiny, and
consequently the fate of all posterity through his intercessory role, or mission in their behalf, as it were, was placed
in his own hands.

This conditional aspect of divine revelation (prophecy) regarding Adam's test and destiny is vital to an understanding of Apocalypse as derived from the story of
our first parents. Such a divine testing of Adam would not

have been possible except that it be commensurate to the human spirit. In this way Adam's whole being was alerted to avoid the danger at hand. The point is, even though the serpent finally enticed him to gaze on the fruit, and Eve swayed his better judgment, they did not budge his instinctive reluctance to transgress the will of God. (Notice the guilty Adam instinctively hiding himself from God the minute he fell from grace.) O happy fault that Adam's vulnerable human nature qualified him for the mercy of God! "For God hath concluded all in unbelief that he may have mercy on all" (Rom 11:32).

Parenthetically, this may explain why Bible fundamentalists failed to recognize the true nature of the Book of Revelation as a conditional prophecy. Since they can admit of no spiritually endowed Church mission (Catholicism) as having been divinely endowed to intermediate mankind's cause within the divine plan, in, through and by Christ, they could never visualize any other fate for the world save what they perceive as the Book of Revelation's inevitable "prophecy of doom." Adam was accountable for the world's fate, however, but only insofar as he was accountable for mankind's direct and unconditional access to Paradise.

Put in another way, Adam's accountability for mankind's direct access to Paradise was also his divine calling, or prerogative—a prerogative conditionally prophesied to be in jeopardy of an apocalyptic ending. Hence, we back into a clue to the language of the Book of Revelation in that it conditionally prophesied a world's, and not the world's cataclysmic ending.

This bears directly on the third element essential to the definition of Apocalypse as displayed in the story of

Adam's test. We see in Genesis 3:15, how quickly God came to Adam's rescue by admonishing the serpent: "I will put enmities between thee and the woman, and thy seed and her seed: she shall crush thy head, and thou shalt lie in wait for her heel." In essence it was a pledge of predilection by God to Adam that through his seed, Christ, mankind would avenge Satan's victory over him. His lost paradise would be regained—in the form of Church unity in Christ's completed mystical body. This rests on the doctrine of mankind's promised ultimate spiritual union in Christ's (the "second Adam") Mystical Body, the Church: "There shall be one fold and one shepherd" (John 10:16).

Adam's loss of Paradise, therefore, was apocalyptic, but only in the sense that a world, namely, the world's direct and unconditional access to an earthly paradise was irrevocably compromised away.

Second Apocalypse

Therefore, the continuity of Adam's displaced intercessory role (for regaining paradise directly and unconditionally) was maintained by God's turning to the House of Israel. Taken in this context, the world's future fate next hinged on the outcome of Israel's Mosaic test of faith. But alas, due to her overall insufficient response to the grace of her Mosaic calling, her prerogative for channeling the world's direct and unconditional access to Jesus was apocalyptically shattered. And so, for a second time (based on God's pledge to Abraham of Israel's ultimate messianic reward), we see the three elements of apocalypse exhibited. Thus, once again *a* world, Israel's direct Messianic calling, met with an apocalyptic fate—as symbolized by Christ's prediction of the Holy Temple's fiery destruction. The rejected Messiah therefore had but one last recourse when he turned to the Gentiles with a third (Gospel) test to finalize the fulfillment of his Father's will, namely, mankind's reconciliation with one another in, through and by Christ as Head of his completed mystical body, the Church—which he founded on Peter with a pledge of invincibility against the gates of Hell. This is in keeping with God's pledge of final victory over Satan through Adam's seed. Each component within this human life-long drama (i.e. Adam, Israel, Catholicism) was given a mark of divine predilection as intermediary for the completion of Christ's mission of unity, *directly* and *unconditionally*.

To sum up, we suggest that in spite of the Church's predilection ("There shall be one fold and one shepherd") over Satan, an area of conditionality remained concerning Catholicism's direct or indirect attainment of that final victory. We note the margin for delay, for example, in St. Paul's exhortation: "The God of peace crush Satan under your feet speedily" (Rom 16:20). Catholicism could not afford to treat its gospel prerogative willy-nilly. It had the previous example of its predecessor, the House of Israel, on how a chosen peoples' covenant with God and direct unconditional access to the divine New Covenant of Christ could be compromised and punitively delayed.

St Paul emphasized the conditionality of Israel's direct access to Christ—and consequently, the conditionality of Christ's redemptive death on a cross—when he stated (1 Cor 2:5-8) that Israel's faith stood on the wisdom of men rather than on the power of God: "Howbeit we speak wisdom among the perfect: yet not the wisdom of this world, neither of the princes of this world that come to nought. But we speak the wisdom of God in a mystery, a wisdom which is hidden, which God ordained before the world, unto our glory: Which none of the princes of this world knew; for, if they had known it, they would never have crucified the Lord of Glory!"

Third Apocalypse

Not that Christ could be crucified again, but Catholicism too was given (in Christianity's Gospel test) its own personal set of warning signals as found in the inspired pages of the Book of Revelation. This Book's intrinsic value as an apocalypse lay in its potential to inspire Christianity instinctively to adhere (at least to a sufficient degree) to God's Commandments. This agency of grace (Apocalypse) in no way diminished the providential goodness and mercy of God. On the contrary, such an instinctive adherence to God manifests an even greater depth of providential care providing Catholicism with a built-in alarm system in its calling to complete Christ's mystical body directly ("speedily") through a sufficiently *loving* response (condign merit) to the Church's mustard seed gospel prerogative.

Insofar as Catholicism ignored that final warning signal, the unreached masses became victimized (through fallen human nature) by their own self-inflicted proclivity toward genocide—a fate which Our Lady of Fatima urgently warned the Church not only to prevent, but end once and for all through the Church's last chance for Traditional Church reform. The resulting world-wide weight of human suffering speaks for itself. Today, mercifully, this alternate providential stimulus for conversion Our Lady advised us to avoid is painfully and systematically being applied both to us Catholics and to the world's all but shepherdless humanity. Ironically we live in a world seemingly headed in opposite directions, that of utter chaos, and that of Christian solidarity with Christ—with equal intensity.

In addition, as if this painful indirect access into the "millennial" process of world conversion to Christ were not punishment enough for Catholicism's sin of omission, such a gratuitous victory over Satan leaves the Church vulnerable to his "mystery of iniquity" by way of a concession to him conditionally prophesied in the Book of Revelation. Accordingly, Satan's planned seduction of Catholicism's prerogative over him was the key or "mystery of iniquity" for his being permitted ("unchained") by God to instigate a "revolt" by his "man of sin" during the Church's undetermined period (symbolically, "millennial" period) of indoctrination and reconciliation of mankind with one another in Christ. Satan's cataclysmic uprising would be brief, "for the sake of the elect," however, during which time he would be personally vanquished by Christ. And so, not the physical earth, but "the world, the flesh, and the devil" would end on that fiery note—making way for the second coming of Christ in his capacity as Judge of the living and the dead.

Taken in this perspective, we begin to see how it was Israel's potential mission within the Church (the prefigured messianic kingdom) that the Old Testament prophets revealed in cataclysmic language as susceptible to forfeiture. As often as the periodically hard-hearted Israelites systematically slaughtered the prophets themselves, the Old Testament revealed their obduracy to be on a collision course with the ultimate sin of deicide—a sin which only Israel was capable of committing.

It was only natural for Christ to borrow the apocalyptic language of the Old Testament (during his last discourse to his disciples) when he predicted Israel's Mosaic world would soon be terminated—burnt to a cinder. He indicated that her lost prerogative of meriting the world's direct and unconditional access to the Messiah had already reduced the Jews to a subservient dependence on the Gentile inheritors of the Church's Gospel mission of unity. (That the Old Testament apocalypses, or types, stirred up the Jewish imagination is quite evident by the periodic bands of local doomsday prophets during, before and following Christ's time. They parlayed the conditional prophecies of Jeremiah, Ezekiel, Daniel and others literally into predictions of imminent world destruction).

But since Israel was not to be forever cut off from her rejected Messiah, "For the gifts and calling of God are without repentance" (Rom 11:29), all she lost was the Mosaic privilege of discovering the sweet yoke and light burden of Christ's Gospel mission to mankind. "Behold your house shall be left to you desolate" (Luke 13:35).

Her punishment would be a temporary blindness ("blindness in part"). The blindness would be lifted, but not directly through a hearing of the Gospel, or even for that matter, through the grace of a fear-stimulated soul-searching, such as would prove beneficial (providentially speaking) to the Gentiles in need of such a drastic prodding toward the light of divine truth. But Israel's blindness would be lifted through the divine humbling prod of "emulation of the Gentiles," which is to say, through an attraction to Christianity's "millennial" fruition of the Gospel in Christ. In other words, such a process of conversion through emulation could only take place during "the fullness of the Gentiles:"

"For if thou were cut out of the wild olive tree, which is natural to thee; and, contrary to nature, were grafted into the good olive tree; how much more shall they that are the natural branches, be grafted into their own olive tree? For I would not have you ignorant, brethren, of this mystery, (lest you should be wise in your own conceits), that blindness in part has happened in Israel, until the fullness of the Gentiles should come in. And so all Israel should be saved" (Rom 11:24-26). As for the degree of guilt of the "princes of this world" for crucifying the Lord, the dying Christ himself asked the Father to forgive them, for they knew not what they did. And yet the enormity of the sufferings experienced by the exiled Jewish race these last 2000 years indicates their punishment fits the enormity of the degree of intransigence exhibited by their forefathers.

It is true that those "princes" did not perceive the full nature of their sin (apostasy) with an intellectual awareness such as angels possess. Otherwise they and their misled people would never have been eligible for pardon. But that those scribes and pharisees ("of this world") possessed a high degree of intuition of their guilt—and this is the basis of their apocalyptic downfall—is quite evident, as Scripture points out, by their obdurate reaction to Christ's overwhelmingly manifest miracles, compounded by his

chiding remarks and public exposé of their shallow lives.
Israel's painful and embarrassing transferal of her
messianic calling was bequeathed to the Gentiles who
themselves were then bolstered by their solidarity with
Adam's seed, the Word made flesh, from whom they inherited the Church's Gospel mission and prerogative for
a direct and unconditional victory over Satan's "mystery
of iniquity" or plan against the Church. Satan's plan, simply put, against the "woman in the desert" (Apoc 12:6)
was to infiltrate Christianity's very providential agency (the
Church's Gospel prerogative) against him...not that he
could crush the Church, but that he might plant the apocalyptic seeds of disruption, which is to say, gain access to
the Church's final period of victory over him. In other
words, the Church's Gospel prerogative for a direct entrance into an unconditional final victory over Satan could
be compromised away by her members' insufficient response to the Church's Gospel mission to the world.

The significance of this chink in the Church's armor
is two-fold. First of all, Catholicism's compromised Gospel response would, at its appointed time (i.e. point of no
return) in salvation history, necessitate an alternate providential agency for stimulating mankind's reconciliation
process within Christ's mystical body, the Church. This
very alternate agency, an agency of fear and religious inse-
curity is what Our Lady (the woman in the desert) warned
the Church about at Fatima, which she epitomized as "Russia." She epitomized this agency as "the evils of Russia,"
an all-encompassing world disintegration ultimately leading to the "conversion of Russia," which is to say, conversion of the world to Mary's Immaculate Heart, symbolizing
the Church's final victory over Satan.

But secondly, this alternate providential aid (i.e. "evils of Russia") to the Church's Gospel mission to mankind insured Satan one last exhibition of cataclysmic fury within the Church's "millennial" victory over him before being crushed quickly by Jesus Christ, "for the sake of the elect." In short, the Church's compromised Gospel prerogative broke open the Book of Revelation's protective seal. For, as a conditional prophecy, the Book of Revelation warned the members of the Church from the earliest times not to compromise her Gospel prerogative over him. His all-consuming obsession was to render Apocalypse as a skeleton in the Church's closet.

In closing, a definition of "millennium" might be deduced from all this: a functional and lengthy but indeterminate period of grace following the conclusion of Catholicism's intermediary Gospel test—for completing the Church's divinely promised world-wide charismatic evangelization and unification of mankind in, through and by Christ. The Book of Revelation is very forceful in describing the "chaining" of Satan, not as some vague partial curbing of his powers during Christ's time on earth and during the remainder of the Christian era. Rather, Satan's chaining is definitively described as a completely thorough elimination of his awesome powers, "as a roaring lion seeking whom he might devour." This being the case, his chaining could only take place at the end of the Church Militant's Gospel mission.

Only on the condition of Catholicism's compromised Gospel mission, however, was Satan to be "chained" and later "loosed for a little while." "And an angel cast him into the abyss, and closed and sealed it over him, that he should deceive the nations no more, until the thousand years should be finished. And after that he must be let loose for a little time" (Apoc 20:3).

II

OUR LADY OF FATIMA
AND THE LOURDES CONNECTION

The Old Testament not only gives us a clue to the Book of Revelation: its whole theme weaves two interconnected apocalyptic precedents into the Book of Revelation's eschatologic fabric. Insofar as Catholic commentators have failed to focus on this Old Testament theme, their remissness helps to explain their reserve at the mention of "the signs of the times." Their failure to recognize the Old Testament's use of conditional prophecy adds to their difficulty.

Three successive participants constitute Holy Scripture's theme: Adam, Israel and the Catholic Church, as mankind's providentially established human intermediaries with God in salvation history. Each of these intermediaries in turn was divinely gifted, through the anticipated merits of Christ in the case of Adam, with a prerogative for *directly and unconditionally* fulfilling its calling in behalf of mankind's salvation process. And so, when God successively warned each of these intermediaries by way of conditional prophecies (divine revelation, or apocalypse) not to compromise mankind's spiritual fate, it was in reference to the apocalyptic loss of a prerogative.

Thus, a thread of guilt weaves its way through the Catholic Church's compromised Gospel prerogative touching on mankind's divinely promised unification in Christ. It was a prerogative inherited by the Christian

Gentiles at the expense of the House of Israel's similar (Mosaic) prerogative of faith for the entering of both Israel and the gentiles directly and unconditionally into Christ's Messianic gospel mission of unity. In turn, it was a prerogative which had been divinely bestowed on Israel at the expense of Adam's compromised intermediary test of obedience (paradise lost). But it happened that both Adam and Israel survived the guilt of their compromised intercessory missions to mankind by virtue of God's irrevocable promise to them (through Adam's seed) of a share in Christ's redemptive victory over Satan. Nevertheless, both paid the maximum punitive price for failing to heed God's ominous warning. Both lost *a* world, namely, their intermediary grace for attaining the world's direct and unconditional access to Christian unity in Christ.

Since the Old Testament could not conditionally prophecy beyond the outcome of Israel's Mosaic test of faith, a separate source of conditional prophecy (the Book of Revelation) had to be divinely inspired as a warning to Catholicism not to compromise the Church's intermediary gospel mission to mankind.

This means that for the Book of Revelation to have had any moral basis for projecting apocalyptic upheavals upon mankind, such prophecies, or types had to be conditionally dependent upon Catholicism's Gospel test aided by the Church's special intermediary Gospel prerogative initially gifted in due season, to project a sufficiently authentic Christian image charismatically endowed to attract all of mankind in, through and by Christ into a direct and unconditional triumph over Satan. In other words, Satan's direct and unconditional "chaining" was conditionally prophesied as susceptible to a brief but cataclysmic "unchaining." But why, we may ask, is the loss of such a power over Satan's eschatological activities compared to an "end of the world" theme? Because this theme was employed by Christ himself when he described Israel's painful (although temporary) banishment from the New Jerusalem, the Church. For there is no more graphic way to describe the consequences of Israel's lost Messianic opportunity.

Plainly, the Book of Revelation did not reveal a battle between Satan and Jesus Christ, for that would have been no contest. But Satan could garner from its pages that a concession was available to his scheming assault, "like a roaring lion," against the Church's Gospel potential for cutting his evil plan short. This fits in with Satan's masterminding of Catholicism's insufficient Gospel response. Although the Church's final victory over Satan was never at risk, Catholicism's Gospel legacy left open which of two providential scenarios the Church's unification of mankind would be attained, (a) directly and unconditionally, or (b) punitively and with eschatological overtones. In the latter scenario, Our Lady of Fatima's reference to the "evils of Russia" involved the reduction of Catholicism's spiritually neglected world into dire straits.

If we can visualize the timing of Mary's Fatima apparitions as providentially critical to the condition of the Church's Christian image (or 2000 years' Gospel legacy), then her urgent requests for Church reform take on an added (eschatological) meaning. For example, her two stipulations for "peace" are significant. Her first *if clause* regarding the Church's long overdue need for thorough reform guaranteed unconditional peace to the world: "If my requests are granted, Russia will be converted and there will be peace." But, had not Mary added yet another *if clause* to her stipulation for peace, one that guaranteed only a qualified period of peace, we would never have guessed the eschatological significance she was giving to "Russia," or to "Russia's conversion," or to "peace."

Why was Mary's message of peace qualified then, except in the context of the Book of Revelation's conditionally prophesied eschatological interruption of Church unification, as expressed by the "unchaining" of Satan? "If my requests are not granted, Russia will spread its errors throughout the world raising up wars and persecutions against the Church. Many will be annihilated. In the end, my Immaculate Heart will triumph and a *period of peace* will be given to mankind."

To sum up, therefore, the Fatima generation's insufficient response to the Church's last chance for acquiring world peace (Christian unification in Christ) through traditional reform, shackled the Church's mission with an alternate providentially permitted punitive agency of grace, namely, the world's reduction to a near condition of moral futility in the wake of Soviet Russia's rape of mankind. Unfortunately for the Church, such a punitively gained crisis-motivated conversion of mankind is also strapped with an eschatological proviso, that only the speedy appearance (*parousia*) of a triumphant Christ's second coming will be able to remedy.

What that very favored Fatima generation (1917-1967) failed to realize, therefore, was that traditional Church reform of itself weighed in the balance at Fatima. Up to that time it had been Catholicism's only available spiritual means for renewal throughout the centuries by which it could maintain the Church's Gospel prerogative. In other words, if traditional Church reform went by the wayside, so too would disappear Catholicism's direct and unconditional Gospel prerogative for attaining Satan's direct and unconditional defeat.

This can only lead to the conclusion that Mary's apparitions at Fatima addressed the Church at the "acceptable time" of Gospel accountability for its mustard seed calling over Satan in salvation history. At that historic moment a whole Catholic generation (the Fatima generation) was made accountable for the Church's 2000 years' Gospel legacy. The Church was exhorted to respond—at least to a sufficient degree—to Mary's urgent last chance invitation for utilizing its intermediary Gospel advantage over Satan's "mystery of iniquity." In short, Catholicism's sufficient response to the Fatima message of peace would have obviated the opening of Vatican II (as the Church's entrance point into mankind's final days of unification in Christ). Taken in this sense, Mary's pivotal hortative role to the Church paralleled Our Lord's hortative role to "his Father's house," during Israel's Messianic "acceptable time."

Hence, the Church's traditional reform movement is not an issue here—as though it should be re-established at the expense of Vatican II. The intriguing quality of Vatican II is that it providentially adjusted the Church's mission to mankind, so to speak, so as to adapt it to the changing times. But this, at the same time, is its weakness. The subtlety here is that it isn't the Church that should have changed for the times—it is the times that should have changed commensurately with a growing church. Once Catholicism's insufficient growth-rate allowed the times to get out of hand, it became providentially expedient for the Church to mitigate "the more excellent way" St. Paul spoke of. . . by a temporary double standard, if you will. For example, Moses began handing out bills of divorce, but only as a gentler providential remedy for his people's hardness of heart. The culprit, therefore, is not Vatican II, as not a few arch-conservatives would have us to believe. In retrospect, Vatican II reforms have successfully addressed some of the areas responsible for the real culprit: pre-Vatican II's insufficiently formed Christian image.

And so it happened that three Portuguese children echoed the traditional requirements of Church reform in the simple language of youngsters: "Do penance, avoid doing bad things, pray the rosary, etc." The question arises, however, what impact would their simple witness have had upon their society without an assist from "the Miracle of the Sun?" The prodigious signs and wonders performed by Jesus Christ himself answer this question by the precedent he set for church reform: "Otherwise believe for the very works' sake" (John 14:12). We have but to recall with nostalgia the venerable names and works of saintly church reformers and founders of religious orders to realize what an enormous supernatural tradition has quietly dried up within our Church's apostolic cause since the opening of Vatican II.

Oddly enough, an unfavorable comparison is made between the miracles of Lourdes and the Fatima episode, so as to downplay the latter. While the miracles of Lourdes continue to impress us all, the pious happenings at Fatima, bolstered by an unconvincing "miracle of the dancing sun," are quietly relegated by the Church itself to a nebulous category of private revelation. It might help, however, not to compare Lourdes with Fatima, but to connect Our Lady's role at Lourdes as a supporting role to our Lady's culminating role at Fatima.

To put it into an equation, Mary's role to the Church emerged at Lourdes as that of "the second Eve." She proclaimed herself in such terms: "I am the Immaculate Conception." It is at Lourdes that so many wounds of struggling mankind are being washed in healing waters. Yet, the continued spiritual productivity of that revered shrine may have had an added function: that of establishing the Immaculate heart of Mary's spiritual credentials in preparation for her hortative role at Fatima, during Catholicism's "acceptable time" of Gospel accountability. As suggested above, Our Lady of Fatima's hortatory role to the Church paralleled Our Lord's hortative role to the House of Israel at the "acceptable time" of its Mosaic mediatory test of faith. He openly proclaimed himself as the "light of the world." His Messianic credentials for this claim (as the second Adam) were established during his public life through a prodigious display of miracles to the lame, the halt, and the blind, to such a degree as to challenge Israel's incredulity. The point to be made here, however, is that he challenged (Israel's) incredulity; he didn't overwhelm it.

(And it is in this vein that we compare Lourdes with Fatima). For example, Christ's raising Lazarus from the dead openly exposed the incredulous House of Israel as

having reached the point of no return regarding its Mosaic prerogative of faith in Jesus (for entering mankind
directly and unconditionally into Christian unity). Thus,
when he was mockingly challenged by the Temple leaders
to perform one more miracle—"bring down manna from
heaven as Moses had done, and we will believe"—he could
easily have overwhelmed them by submitting to their sug-
gestion. But that would have been counter productive to
the challenge of faith implicit in their Mosaic calling. So
too, Fatima's seemingly unconvincing "miracle of the sun"
witnessed by 70,000 people on a cold, misty, miserable
day, could have been followed up by such an awesome display of miracles beyond those of Lourdes so as to overwhelm even the Church itself into establishing it as an ar-
ticle of faith. That, of course, would have been counter
productive to our Lady's hortative role to Catholicism at
the critical time of its point of no return for utilizing its
Gospel responsibility of faith (for entering mankind directly and unconditionally into the completion of Christ's
mystical body, the Church).

Ironically, we live in a world seemingly headed in opposite directions with equal intensity: that of utter chaos,
and that of Christian solidarity. It is no longer the threat
from Soviet Russia that concerns us, however, but the in-
creasingly desperate human condition left in the wake of
Communism's great atheistic experiment. Sad to say,
Russia's raping of the world has managed to affect adversely
mankind's spirituality both directly and indirectly. This is
no small achievement, for it meant placing a wedge between the Gospel Truth and mankind's tenuous hold on
self-evident truths. Such was the concern of Our Lady of

Fatima. She warned the Church that God's *modus operandi* for Christian unity (Catholicism's special intercessory Gospel responsibility for directly attracting mankind into the One True Fold of Christ) could be (punitively) substituted for by an alternate fear-induced *modus operandi*. God is quite capable of stimulating the hearts of men reduced, by their own folly, to dire straits—such as happened during the Deluge: Long-suppressed lights and ignored self-evident truths—such as have been divinely deposited in one degree or another into the consciences of all men— can be aroused by the grace of a painful and bitter awakening process.

This punitive *modus operandi* for stirring up mankind's spiritual awareness may well explain Catholicism's post-Vatican II queasy experience of crisis-spirituality, combined as it is, with another crisis of numbers within the Church's divinely called priestly and religious harvesters. St. Paul once posed a rhetorical question: "Or how shall they believe him, of whom they have not heard? And how shall they hear, without a preacher?" (Rom 10:14). And Christ himself hinted that where the harvesters are few, the responsibility for an increase of vocations lay not entirely with God: "Pray ye therefore the Lord of the harvest, that he send forth laborers into the harvest" (Matt 9:38).

No wonder Satan "stood upon the sand of the sea!" in his crafty maneuvering. The very rivers from the dragon's mouth that would prove ineffective against the Church's foundation, would be effective against the Church's "offspring" (individual Catholics) so as to cause them to compromise away the Church's unconditional Gospel power over his seductive powers. This being the case, the "earth" (seduced humanity), having been denied the Church's direct and unconditional Gospel mission to them, would become even more vulnerable to the dragon's rivers of moral degradation. But there, by the grace of God, is where the "earth helps the woman," in that the rivers from the dragon's mouth are made to act as a source of spiritual awakening for the earth's deadened consciences and repressed knowledge of God.

Thus, the woman will become the beneficiary of the earth's piteous cries for help. The woman, in return, will gently respond (ecumenically, by way of a painfully evolved mitigated spiritual dispensation) commensurate with the earth's stunted and emaciated capacity for divine Truth. And so, Our Lady of Fatima's projection of her Immaculate Heart puts a finishing touch to this picture. For, just as Christ's eventual victory over Satan will be effected through his completed Mystical Body, the Church, so will Mary's powerful mediation crush Satan's head under her foot (Gen 3:15) so as to finalize her divine Son's completed mission to his Father on earth.

What might have been Mary's role in the Church had the House of Israel sufficiently responded to Christ's gospel calling? Even as the stage for Israel's entrance into the "New Jerusalem" (the Church) was being set, the angel Gabriel was saluting the Virgin Mary as "full of grace." And, as that very docile but "troubled" young girl pondered her own natural shortcomings, she was reassured that, "The Holy Spirit shall come upon thee and the power of the most High shall overshadow thee. And therefore also the Holy which shall be born of thee shall be called the Son of God." (Luke 1).

At that point of time in salvation history, Mary's fiat initiated a favored role within the yet to be established Church. For, although her consent was in total conformity with the House of Israel's Mosaic test of faith, its intrinsic significance transcended Israel's eventual rejection of the Church's Messianic Cornerstone. This is borne out by the divinely inspired words of Elizabeth, her cousin and kindred spirit: 'Blessed art thou among women, and blessed is the fruit of thy womb." To which Mary responded, "My soul doth magnify the Lord ...for behold from henceforth all generations shall call me blessed" (Luke 1:48). It is quite evident today that the universal Church's devotional Marian perpetuation throughout "all generations", stems from the angel Gabriel's first Ave Maria and has transcended the Holy Temple's Messianic impasse.

We may recall that Christ's first ministry to the House of Israel was to formally give notice that the time for accountability (the acceptable time) of its Mosaic test of faith had arrived. The New Jerusalem was awaiting, so to speak, the Temple's apocalyptic determination. To be determined, therefore, was Israel's direct and unconditional smooth transition into the Church's gospel mission to mankind. That is to say, Israel's gospel prerogative as charter members of Christ's redemptive mission to mankind would have liberated the Church from the spectre of yet another apocalyptic threat, such as that found in the Book of Revelation. And it follows from this, Satan's "mystery of iniquity" would be rendered inconceivable. This is not to say the Church's Christocentric apostolate would become a matter of ease. For, Satan's opposition would be fierce as ever, even perhaps to the extent of flowing rivers of martyr's blood. But his time would be cut short by the Church's gradual ecumenical transformation into the image of Christ. This, in turn, would obviate our Lady's urgent eschatologic hortatory role to the Church which prompted her apparitions at Fatima. At any rate, during the last days, within the exigency of the Church, prophetically speaking, a woman's foot will crush the head of the very serpent whose guile had precipitated God's first humiliating onus upon our mother, Eve, and all womankind conceived in sin.

Mary's apocalyptic role, then, is best clarified by raising the question: Why, was she present in the Cenacle receiving the Holy Spirit's tongues of fire along with Christ's selected Apostles at the conception of the Church? Was she there in order to receive a greater abundance of grace--she who already had been given a plenitude of grace? She who had been overshadowed by the power of the most High? Or was she there by virtue of her fullness of grace, to assume a potential role in the Church relevant to the apocalyptic outcome of Catholicism's yet to be tested gospel mission of faith? It would be a role uniquely tailored to Mary by reason of her unique relationship to Jesus. For, only the Immaculate Heart of a heavenly advocate such as the Mother of God could supplement the Sacred Heart of Jesus in his compassionate, hortative and prophetic (apocalyptic) role to the House of Israel. That is to say, only a heavenly advocate such as Our Lady of Fatima could have adequately supplemented the Father's apocalyptic grace to Adam, the Son's apocalyptic grace to Israel and the Holy Spirit's apocalyptic grace to Catholicism.

III

THE BOOK OF REVELATION

In the Book of Revelation, not one but two complete apocalypses are presented as viewed from two distinct preoccupations. H. B. Swete writes: "With the seventh trumpet-blast the kingdom of God had come, and the general judgment is at hand. Thus, this section of the Apocalypse (chapters 4-11) brings the course of history down to the verge of the Parousia. If the Book had ended here, it would have been within these limits complete. But the Seer pauses for a moment only to take up his role again with a fresh presentation of the future, in which the vision is to be carried to its issue. Impelled by a fresh gift of prophetic energy, he feels himself bound to prophesy again to a larger circle of hearers and with wider aims (Apoc 10:11); and this second message occupies the remainder of the Book."[1]

St. John was preoccupied in the first section, or apocalypse (Apoc 4-11), with the Church's relationship to the chosen people. He wrote it as though it preceded in time his measuring of the temple (the Church) and the casting out of the outer court (the synagogue)... "It is given over to the nations, and they will trample over the holy city for forty-two months" (Apoc 11:2). This first apocalypse, however, with its series of seals and trumpets is no more than a development of the data of Christ's discourse in Matt. 24, sometimes called the synoptic apocalypse. "The destruc-

---

[1]H.B. Swete, *The Apocalypse of St. John*, London, 1922. III, xxxix, 5.

tion of Jerusalem and its sanctuary was not the end of the world but it was the end of a world. It marked the definitive separation of synagogue and Church. Henceforth, the latter turned principally to the Gentiles."[2]

The historical setting of the second apocalypse (12-22) is the coming persecution of the Church by Rome, and the precise occasion of the persecution is the Church's refusal to countenance Caesar-worship; the two Beasts represent Rome and the religion of Rome. These pages attack the blasphemous pretensions of the emperors, which must end in disaster: Rome will go the way of Babylon.

The Jews had their destiny as well as that of Jerusalem in their own hands. Their predicted synoptic apocalyptic fate could have been avoided. They were destined to receive the kingdom of heaven, the Church... but it was temporarily denied them and transferred to the Gentiles: "Be it known therefore to you that this salvation of God is sent to the Gentiles, and they will hear it" (Acts 28:28). There is an inherent connection between destiny and good works. That which was temporarily lost to the Jews happened because they allowed their own destiny to slip through their hands. They were called to become "a perfect people," but ended up by being "blinded in part."

The first apocalypse ends by revealing the "mystery of God" (Apoc 10:7), or man's incorporation in the mystical Body of Christ. Now this deified union would place the Church's destiny, and that of the world in the Church's own hands. The Church in growing union with its head

---

[2]It is a revival of Augustine's tentative opinion (PL 33, 904-25). A. Feuillet, *Johannine Studies*, New York: Alba House, 1964. op. cit. 229f.

was called to defeat Satan outright. How perfect should this growing union of the members of the Church be with its head? This brings us back to the notion of "perfection." St. John does not write: Blessed are the dead who receive the hundredfold, or sixty-fold...but he writes: "Blessed are the dead who die in the Lord...for their works follow them" (Apoc 14:13). This refers not only to martyrs but to all the faithful. He was not concerned at the moment about individual degrees of glory. The sufficient performance of good works insofar as they aid the faithful in the salvation of their own souls qualifies them as "perfect." But, more importantly by this perfection they make a lasting contribution to the normal growth of the mystical Body of Christ: "their works follow them."

If but a bare minimum of true Christians "die in the Lord" the Church, along with the world for whom it is responsible, will attain the cherished potential, or destiny of unconditional victory over Satan. The "mystery of God," (the Mystical Body of Christ) will evangelize (subdue the earth) without delay (unconditionally): "And the angel, whom I saw standing upon the sea and upon the earth, lifted up his hand to heaven, and the things which are therein; and the earth, and the things which are in it; and the sea, and the things which are therein: That time (delay) shall be no longer. But the days of the voice of the seventh angel, when he shall begin to sound the trumpet, the mystery of God shall be finished, as he has declared by his servants (evangelists) the prophets" (Apoc 10:5-7).

St. John wrote from the vantage point of both the demise of the Old Jerusalem, and the birth of the New Jerusalem. He measured the temple with a reed (Apoc

11:1), modeled on Ez. 40; 43:13-17, and Zach. 2, where the "new" all-holy Jerusalem is measured for preservation and purification. (The essential Church shall not perish even during world-persecution.) The People (Church as a "lamp" Apoc 11:4) would be fed by the oil of two olive trees. "But the court, which is without the temple, cast out, and measure it not: because it is given unto the Gentiles, and the holy city they shall tread under foot two and forty months:" (Apoc 11:2). Which is to say: the holy city Jerusalem would be given up to pagan desecration.

Two witnesses standing before the Lord would constantly remind Jerusalem of its apostasy. The Jews had Elias who could "shut up the heavens" (Lk 4:25), and Moses brought plagues on Egypt. The temporal "death" of the two witnesses, as though by a Wild beast from the Abyss (Apoc 11:7) would signify Jewish "blindness in part," who no longer were gnawed by the guilt of having rejected these two witnesses, Elias and Moses. "And their bodies shall lie in the streets of the great city, which is called spiritually, Sodom and Egypt, where their Lord also was crucified" (Apoc 11:8). Jerusalem was, for St. John, the Great Apostate. The world had depended on the fate of Jerusalem; now the fate of Jerusalem depended on the world. John had seen the world, which should have been the all Holy City, or Holy Land, turned into the wickedest of cities, Sodom, and the lands of Egypt—nay into one vast Calvary.

The overall effort of the chosen people fell short of their accountability to their mission of "perfection" or preparation for their Messiah. Their compromised direct (Mosaic) access to Christ would then be temporarily sidetracked by "blindness in part." It follows that the Old Testament prophecy of a permanent Messianic reign could no longer occur (for the Jews) at the completion of Christ's mission to them. It (Old Testament prophecy) was, therefore, a conditional prophecy dependent upon Israel's calling to "perfection."

St. John was a prophet in that a detailed pattern was revealed to him of victory by the young Church over the terrible persecutions that Rome was about to unleash. But in writing of that situation, he had no prophetical insight as to a world-ending conflict between Right and Wrong. His vision consisted essentially of the efficacy of the blood of martyrs for procuring the unconditional defeat of pagan Rome. His main concern was the survival of the contemporary Church. He was not necessarily aware that this struggle was to be a prototype of the Church Militant's struggle for an unconditional victory over Satan.

St. John was exiled to Patmos. Powerful Rome and infant Christianity were on a collision course. Roman spies and informers were everywhere. Clairvoyance, however, was on the side of John. His vision had to be smuggled out to the Christian communities, and it was a divinely inspired source of hope, a fortifier of faith and a warning for all to watch against apostasy. His symbolism, or revelation added nothing new to the deposit of faith. He had no special insight concerning the last days of mankind on earth. Yet he was intuitively aware that anyone altering his words would be foolishly tampering with some mysteriously significant pattern of the future.

By likening Old Testament situations to the perilous days of the infant Church, and even by culling the language of Jewish apocalyptic writings to fit the situation at hand, St. John could smuggle out under the Roman noses, the divinely revealed strategy of the Church's triumph over imperial Rome. How better to couch his message from hostile eyes than by the use of pertinent phraseology from Old Testament prophets? A case could be made that the imagery and method of St. John's Apocalypse are not derived from any special revelation or visions granted the apostle, but rather from the use of current literary form for the expression of religious truth. For example, John's "Rome" is Jeremiah's "Babylon": a cesspool of luxury, lust, and idolatry. Jeremiah would write: "Babylon: is suddenly fallen and destroyed" (51:8).

The inference here to the fall of Rome would be unmistakably clear to the trembling Christians. St. John borrowed another bit of imagery from Daniel's "dragon," to describe "the dragon, the ancient serpent who is the devil and Satan" (Apoc 20. 2). "I looked, and lo: there was a fourth beast dreadful and terrible...it had ten horns...and some of the starry host it cast down to the ground and trampled underfoot" (Dan 7:7).

Although the dragon's wrath against the woman (or Church) in the desert is somewhat checked (Apoc 12:16), his might is nevertheless directed against the people of God. John's beast out of the sea (12:3) is a counterpart of Satan, with ten horns and ten diadems which Daniel described well as Satan's consummate evil might. This beast from across the sea, was Rome: "It appeared like a leopard...feet like a bear...mouth speaking great things" (Dan 7:20). St. John employed this imagery of blasphemous names emanating from the beast to represent the emperor worship and the emperors' use of titles such as "savior of the world," "son of God," etc. St. John saw one of the heads "smitten as it were unto death, but its deadly wound was healed" (Apoc 13:3). This bit of originality depicted what Christ had already revealed, namely, continual hostility through the centuries toward the Church by secular governments. But perhaps, too, it alluded to the legend of Nero's so-called return from death. The "name of the beast, or the number (666) of its name" also could be cleverly attributed to Nero, or Caesar (13:17).

When he envisions Satan chained for a thousand years (20:1), he is in effect painting a rosy picture of the reward awaiting the soon-to-be martyred in Christ, as untouchable by Satan. At the same time he is praising their contribution towards the Church's future reward: a partial mitigation of Satan's power.

The manner in which St. John incorporated Jewish eschatological speculations is perhaps the clue to the added two-dimensional, or "typical" scope of the Book of Revelation. An interesting development began taking place among Jewish writers shortly before the coming of Christ. Seeing the effects of the ravages of sin and the hopelessness of world tyranny and debauchery, they began to waver in their expectations of a permanent Messianic reign. They speculated upon a temporary Messianic reign followed by an eschatologic combat and world-ending conflict between Right and Wrong. No doubt the threat of Rome heightened these speculations.

Although there was no reason for St. John to speculate about the last days of the world, he found in Jewish writings a good analogy for the Christian drama about to take place. His inspired vision provided him with the knowledge that the infant Church was to be divinely aided to triumph over Rome. But this in turn meant for him that the Messianic reign was about to begin as a mustard seed. The mystery of the Mystical Body of Christ was opening up to him like a flower. And he had no reason to doubt its potential against the wiles of Satan.

The choice of his words was far from accidental. The Book of Revelation contained a blue-print of Catholic folly paralleling the Old Testament's pattern of Jewish folly. They revealed a potential Christian punishment commensurate with the Jewish punishment of blindness to its lost opportunity of direct access to its Messiah...as well as a potential Christian version of the Jewish shortened messianic kingdom, which is to say, a Christian messianic kingdom interrupted by the "unchaining of Satan." This calculated stimulator of the religious instinct was scripturally inspired for Christians to ponder and decipher through the course of history. Like the Jews, they too could ignore their Messiah to their own detriment. They would learn from it that only their sufficient response to the Gospel message could preserve and develop tranquility of order throughout the world. Otherwise the Christian charter of love begins to be compromised, giving way to its temporary providential replacement, fear, (the instinct of self-preservation) as a salvific contributing factor for completing the Church's unifying mission in Christ. Such a gratuitous providential contributing factor, however, would be just as punishing to the Church in its mission to the world as was the Jewish punishment of "blindness in part."

Jesus, too, used metaphorical language so as not to arouse the wrath of the Synagogue. The symbolism that he used not only indicated that his own sufficiently cooperative Israel could have canceled out the Old Testament's types of Jewish folly, but by the same token, the same symbolism provided a sufficiently cooperative Catholicism with the potential of canceling out the conditional prophecy of Christian folly as revealed in the Book of Revelation. The "mustard seed," could have canceled out the "mystery of iniquity." The "Good Shepherd" could have canceled out the victory of the "ten kings." Yes, the parables of Christ should have canceled out the "dooms and glooms" of the Apocalypse: "The reign of God is like yeast which a woman took and kneaded into three measures of flour" (Matt 13:33). This "yeast" was given the potential of canceling out any further activity ("unchaining") of Satan during the world's *unconditional* fruition of the Messianic Kingdom.

Even though the immediate ends of Israel's Mosaic test of faith, followed by Christianity's Gospel test of "putting on Christ" were not identical, the means for fulfilling, or "earning" those two ends were the same, namely, the development of a proper (humble) disposition attained through a sufficient cooperation (condign merit) with God's grace. This meritorious disposition once developed, God, at an appointed time would then utilize it as a secondary cause (through His Son's merits) for the *direct* fulfillment of His will to save all men. "For this is good and acceptable in the sight of God our Savior, who will have all men to be saved, and to come to the knowledge of the truth" (1 Tim 2:3,4). "For God sent not his Son into the world, but that the world may be saved by him" (John 3:17).

By way of analogy, when the House of Israel came face to face with its promised Messiah, the appointed time arrived for him to throw the cup of gasoline (his Gospel message) on the log of Israel's Mosaic test. Had Israel but become properly disposed, through a sufficient response to the grace, or rather, as it were, through the drying-out and heating process of the chosen people's Mosaic calling, she would have become immediately consumed by the gift of his divine light.

Not that Israel's Mosaic calling to the Messiah was to be an end in itself. But a loyal Israel would ride on the wave of her meritorious disposition into the New Jerusalem, the kingdom of heaven, the Church. There would then follow the unfinished business for these new residents of Christ's Messianic reign: to take up his Gospel and complete its potential for drawing all men directly to him—by "putting on Christ." Christ, however, would not require that his loyal followers "carry the Cross" in order to follow him. His only stipulation (before his formal rejection by the Jews) was that his followers bear his "sweet yoke, and light burden" (Matt 11:30), and that they come to him for refreshment. An honest effort in that direction would slowly transform their collective image into an efficacious "image of Christ," empowering them, (and in a much quicker fashion) as authentic Christians, to attract all of mankind into unity in Christ. In this way, Israel's meritorious disposition would be utilized by Christ as a secondary cause for the fulfillment of his promised Church unity..."There shall be one fold and one shepherd"...and directly rewarded by all of mankind's unconditional victory over Satan.

Some might be a bit skeptical that a Christian-formed "image of Christ" can suddenly transform Catholicism into an efficacious instrument for attracting all of mankind into the unity of Christ. For, even the physical presence of the divine Word of God made flesh, along with his plethora of miracles, were not automatically grasped, especially by a recalcitrant Synagogue. It comes down to the question of God's gifts. Both for Jews and Christians, belief in Christ is a gift of God's grace. For the Jews, the grace to respond sufficiently to their Mosaic test of faith provided them with the opportunity of meritoriously forming a disposition, or docility to the truth, primed to receive the saving Gospel of Christ. This meritorious disposition was to be their gate of entrance as charter members into Christ's Church (kingdom of heaven) and its mission to the world.

Had they not rejected Christ, there would have been, of course, no symbolical "Christian Cross" for them to bear. Nevertheless, the world, the flesh and the devil would make sure their application of the Gospel ("putting on Christ") would for the most part be heroic. Their adherence to the Gospel, even to the extent of martyrdom, would be distinguishable from the comparable weight of the Cross inherited by the Gentiles only in that their yoke would be sweetened and their burden lightened by a greater participation of the fruits of the Holy Spirit. Unfortunately for us all, the Jews rejected their Messiah. So, in a sense, Christianity inherited what the Jews failed to merit, namely, Christ's Messianic Kingdom. That is the good news.

The bad news is that Christianity had to merit what the faithful Jews would have inherited, namely, a guaranteed assurance of "putting on Christ" sufficiently ("sufficiently" as in the parable of the Sower, whose seed fell on good ground: "and they brought forth fruit, some an hundredfold, some sixtyfold, and some thirtyfold" (Matt 13:8), and of fulfilling the Gospel's mustard seed prerogative.

And so it happened, Christianity inherited both Christ and his Cross, at the expense of Israel's compromised Mosaic test. The mantle of the world was at that moment shifted to the shoulders of Christianity. Once again the world would have to await the outcome of a test: Christianity's Gospel test of "putting on Christ" sufficiently. It would again have to await the test of a (Christian) log, heated, lo, so many years, by the Gospel test. At an appointed time Christ would come to see if his cup of gasoline (or added spark of grace) would transform Catholicism into the efficacious flame of his image." For, that "image" alone could fulfill the Church's charismatic mustard seed potential for directly attracting all of mankind in, and through and by Christ—and consequently, into an unconditional victory over Satan.

The Bottom Line

Just as he who sees
Christ, sees the Father:
Whom should he see,
Who fixes his eyes
on a Christian -
But all three?

IV

THE SON OF MAN'S LEARNING PROCESS

"And as Moses lifted up the serpent in the desert, so must the Son of man be lifted up: That whosoever believeth in him may not perish; but may have life everlasting" (John 3:14-16). Commentators see "necessity" as a dominant idea in verse 14. They see proclaimed in this passage the necessity of Christ's redeeming death. "Exaltation" is crucifixion. The brazen serpent raised by Moses as a divine remedy for poisonous serpent bite, was a figure of salvation through Christ crucified.

According to this view, Christ, at the very beginning of his public life, is proclaiming to Nicodemus the necessity of his crucifixion as a means of reconciling mankind with God. An opposing thesis, therefore, would be unfounded in holding that Christ, as the Son of man, learned the unraveling of his Father's plan of redemption day by day through an infused knowledge. Such a thesis suggests that even though he studied the Old Testament prophecies pointing to his death at the hands of his own people, they remained for him conditional prophecies contingent upon Israel's final response to its Mosaic test of faith. This seems to be borne out by his frequent protestations that he came, not to judge his own people. This being so, Israel's point of no return did not occur until the Synagogue formally rejected him. In the meantime he worked for the miracle of Nineveh right up until his Father's voice made "Judgment of the world" (John 12:31), which took place towards the end of his public life. "Now is my soul troubled. And what shall I say? Father save me from this hour. But for this cause I came into this hour" (John 12:27). The "cause" he spoke of was his Father's will, and it brought him (through obedience), "unto this hour" of immolation. Not that the Father limited Christ's redemptive act by the extremes of immolation. But (as conditionally prophesied) the Synagogue's formal rejection of Christ was the condition triggering God's alternate plan of redemption, namely, His Son's rejection and crucifixion by the Jews.

The lifting up of the serpent in the desert by Moses, although a figure of Christ's crucifixion, did not, according to other commentators, limit the redemptive act to crucifixion. The figure, or type, of Christ's crucifixion was divinely inscribed in the Old Testament pages as a thinly disguised deterrent to the House of Israel from compromising its Mosaic test—an option of faith endowed to make Israel amenable, or receptive to the "Light of the World," when he appeared. (By the same token, the Book of Revelation acted as a deterrent to the Catholic Church in its Gospel test of faith.) With this in mind, we can shift the dominant idea of the above verses, John 3:14-16, to the thought of Redemption, as closely connected, not to Christ's crucifixion, but to his Incarnation. Whatever requirements the Father willed of Christ, he, by obeying would become a sinless Savior in the likeness of sinful flesh healing the poisoned wounds of sin and giving life everlasting. This would be in keeping with the type of the non-poisonous serpent raised up by Moses, which, when looked upon with faith, healed poisoned wounds and preserved temporal life. In this respect, one drop of Christ's blood

shed in conformity to the Father's will would have sufficed to reconcile all of sinful mankind—through their
belief in his redemptive act—with God.

His Father's will was the source of the Son of man's
exaltation ("raising up"). By his obedience he exalted his
Father, Who in turn exalted him before the multitude when
He permitted it to hear His voice as "thunder" and as an
"angel." "Now is my soul troubled. And what shall I say?
Father, save me from this hour. But for this cause I came
unto this hour. Father, glorify thy name." "A voice therefore came from heaven: 'I have both glorified it, and will
glorify it again.' The multitude therefore that stood and
heard, said that it thundered. Others said: 'An angel spoke
to him.' Jesus answered, and said: 'This voice came not
because of me, but for your sakes. Now is the Judgment of
this world: now shall the prince of this world be cast out'"
(John 12:27,31).

For the Jews, this was their moment of truth; their
Mosaic test was over. The Synagogue's reaction clearly
shows that it understood Christ's meaning as he openly
foretold his crucifixion at the hands of the Jews: "And I, if
I be lifted up from the earth, will draw all men to myself."
(John 12:32) But the subtle point to be made here is that
Jesus, by repeating the prophecy, or type of his being "lifted
up" which he first revealed to Nicodemus at the opening
of his public life in John 3:14-16, completed the double
meaning, or conditional prophecy of the "raising up," or,
"exaltation" of the serpent in the desert. The New Testament makes a remarkable distinction between John 3:14-
16 and John 12:32, in that, following John 12:32, there is
a parenthetic note (John 12:33) which leaves no question

about the nature of Christ's "lifting up," or "exaltation": "(Now this he said, signifying what death he should die.)" Since this parenthetic note (John 12:33) is purposely omitted as an explanation of John 3:14-16, its omission qualifies Christ's original reference to the Son of man's being "lifted up as Moses lifted up the brazen serpent," as a conditional prophecy of his redemptive crucifixion. Hence, John 3:14-16 left Israel with two options, namely, Christ's future "glorification" or "lifting up" through Israel's faithful acceptance of her redeemer's Gospel message; or Christ's future "exaltation" or "lifting up" (crucifixion) through Israel's violent rejection of his Messianic mission to her.

Christ acquired experimental knowledge in the school of experience. He learned the hardness of obedience by obeying through most difficult sufferings even to acceptance of a death involving the utmost pain and shame. "And whereas indeed he was the Son of God, he learned obedience by the things which he suffered" (Heb 5:8). The Word of God did not deem it robbery to be equal with God while taking on the form of a servant (in assuming human nature). His whole life was a learning process, and that is why his humility and meekness have drawn us closer to his Sacred Heart. "And Jesus advanced in wisdom, and age, and grace with God" (Luke 2:52).

On the dogmatic side it may be said that in the incarnate Word were two planes of knowledge—divine and total on one plane, human and limited on the other; direct communication between the two being established only by his supernatural "infused knowledge." This last was infused in proportion to the dignity of the man-God and to the needs of his redemptive work (e.g. knowledge of His own divinity and Messianic character; gift of prophecy). He came to do his Father's will. This was his sacrifice for which a foreknowledge of the "day and hour" of Jerusalem's destruction, or of his second coming was not essential. In keeping with the character and tone of his mission "to the sheep that are lost of the house of Israel" (Matt 15:24), his knowledge of the Jewish destiny was essentially limited to the Old Testament (conditional) prophecies. From those prophecies he learned that until his preaching and miracles met with clear-cut (official) rejection, the Jewish destiny remained in the hands of the House of Israel. So it happened that when the Pharisees had made a serious consultation to destroy him, (Matt 12:14), he immediately recognized (and with true authentic sorrow) the prophetic signals of the fate in store for him and for his beloved people.

At this point the Temple of Jerusalem outdid itself in cleverness, dispatching capable Pharisees and learned Sadducees prepared to request the ultimate sign from heaven. They would liken him to Moses, the greatest of the prophets. They would hope to embarrass him by suggesting that he shower down manna from the heavens, just as Moses had done. Doubtless such a miracle would have impressed them, except that, ironically, this final cynical tempting of the Lord became the House of Israel's point of no return. No longer were these religious leaders worthy of a sign. Their sign was that they had run out of signs. No longer would he warn them. Henceforth he would no longer exhort them. Their brazen insistence on one final spectacular sign from heaven signaled to Christ their repudiation of Nineveh's efficacious example (conversion and penance). There only remained the sign of Jonah in the whale's belly (the type of Christ's death and resurrection) which would painfully reveal his authenticity to the dispersed House of Israel by exposing both his divinity and their act of deicide. It would "convince them of sin." And so he curtly repeated (perhaps in a barely audible whisper) his last warning to them (Matt 12:39), not as a renewed warning, but as a reminder of Israel's lost opportunity. "An evil and unfaithful age is eager for a sign! No sign will be given it but that of the prophet Jonah. And he left them and went away" (Matt 16:4). His Father was calling him to Tabor, yet not for his own benefit, but for that of his disciples. Shortly after his transfiguration the high priest Caiphas rent his garments in an official rejection of Christ by the House of Israel: "It is expedient for you that one man should die for the people, and that the whole nation perish not." (John 11:50).

The Jews forfeited their prerogative as "chicks" (in a later description used by the rejected Master) called directly to the wings of their mother hen. What Israel forfeited was a participation in the choice role of the Church's (the kingdom of heaven's) mission of reconciliation. Consequently, Israel's sin of apostasy denied the world an avenue of direct access into a restored version of Eden also. A Jewish fruition in "putting on Christ" would have graced the House of Israel's sufficient response to its Mosaic test of faith. Its newly acquired authentic "Christian" image, perfected over a period of time through a dogged display of virtue against the ever pernicious world, flesh and devil, would have (as God's intermediary to the world's conversion to Christ) gradually developed into an efficacious garden of delight, an irresistible magnet charismatically endowed to awaken all humanity to "the Way, the Truth and the Life." Instead, this charismatic gospel prerogative was, in the true sense of apocalypse, compromised away only to be transferred to the Gentiles (Catholicism) in the form of a new gospel test. This new test given both to the religious leaders and to all of the members of the Church, was a gospel-calling (obligation) to strive sufficiently to "put on Christ," so that through the agency of his mystical body, Christ might complete his earthly mission of Church unity to his Father, directly and unconditionally (Gal 3:25-29).

It would be a mistake to say that because of God's covenant with Abraham, the Law of Moses put Abraham's promised seed (Christ) on death row, so to speak. The contradiction here is that the disobedience of Adam necessitated the commission of a second transgression (sin of apostasy by Israel). "Why then was the law? It was set because of transgressions until the seed should come, to whom he made the promise, being ordained by angels in the hand of a mediator. Now a mediator is not of one: but God is one" (Gal 3:19,20). "Though this verse (Gal 3:19) might mean that the Law is inferior to the Promise because it comes from God indirectly whilst the Promise comes without intermediary, St. Paul probably means that the Mosaic covenant was a bilateral alliance involving a mediator (Moses) and the possibility of the covenant failing through the transgression of the Jews, whereas God's Promise was unilateral unconditional, indefectible, and could not be modified by the Law. (*A Catholic Commen-*

tary on Holy Scripture, p.1117). The Law of Moses, therefore, was Israel's pedagogue, and a boon for entering a
chosen people directly and unconditionally into Christ's
messianic redemptive mission (the Church) to mankind.
It is true that, according to St. Peter, the divine servant of
the Father was sent on his mission of reconciliation "according to the foreknowledge of God the Father, unto the
sanctification of the Spirit, unto obedience and sprinkling
of the blood of Jesus Christ" (1 Pet 1:2). Yet, as theolo-
gians tell us, Christ's redemptive mission did not require
his complete immolation since one drop of his blood shed
in obedience to his Father's will infinitely sufficed to reconcile mankind to God.

Consequently, the Law of Moses was made the pivotal ingredient in the only set of circumstances through
which the sin of deicide could be committed. This means
that without the intermediary role of Israel, enlightened
as it was by the Law of Moses (Israel's "pedagogue"),
Christ's complete immolation ("obedience unto death")
would never have opened up to him as an option of obedience. But, precisely because the Word of God made flesh
voluntarily subjected himself to the House of Israel's intermediary calling within the mystery of the New Jerusalem (mystical body of Christ, the Church)—which direct
and unconditional Mosaic calling of faith ironically was
made viable through the anticipated grace of Christ's
sprinkled blood—the transgressions (apostasy) of Israel
provided for an emptying out of the Godhead's infinite
love upon mankind through His only begotten Son's "obedience unto death" both as Victim and Priest. And as a
final result, Israel's sin of deicide determined the Spirit of

God's induction of the Gentiles into the Church's direct and unconditional gospel mission to mankind in, by, and through Christ.

V

Obstacle

Christianity is a building process. "Upon this rock I will build my church" (Matt 16). This process of growth was a plan of redemption, a mystery so beneficial to the human condition that if Israel had understood fully what it was getting into, it would have had second thoughts about its opposition to Christ. What followed was a death struggle between the "mystery of iniquity" and the "Mystery." The mystery of iniquity is a power (partially hidden from us) of darkness personified by the prince of darkness operating through the wisdom and power and glory of the flesh. Opposed to him is True Wisdom... "hidden in mystery, ordained of God before the world unto our glory, unknown by all the princes of the world, for, if they had known it, they would not have crucified the Lord of glory" (1 Cor 2:7, 8).

"From this description it appears that divine wisdom has to do with the plan of redemption, and seems to be identical with what St. Paul subsequently calls `The Mystery'—that is to say, the great secret of God in reference to the incorporation of men with Christ in the unity of the mystical body. Like the Mystery, it is hidden in the depths of the divine will; like the Mystery, it has for its object our eternal blessedness; like the Mystery, there was only a glimpse of it in the past, and even the angels knew it only through the medium of the Church, when they contemplated it in its concrete reality ('That the manifold wisdom of God may be made known to the principalities and powers in heavenly places through the Church' [Eph:3:10])...like the Mystery, it can be revealed only by God as by the Spirit which scrutinizes all the secrets of God; and finally, like the Mystery, it is in Jesus Christ that it has its ideal realization."[1]

This was Christ's mission, and it behooves the Son of God to complete his Father's work. "So shall my word be that goes forth from my mouth; it shall not return to me void, but shall do my will, achieving the end for which I sent it" (Is 55:11). For, if Christ, the head of the Church and Savior of his own body (Eph 5:23) attained his fullness of age (4:13), that is to say, the fullness of graces which his title and role require, then it follows that at some point in time the body must become the perfect man. For only the body (not the head) can grow and develop (through the members) in conformity to Christ who is the head. "Until we all meet into the unity of faith and of the knowledge of the Son of God unto a perfect man, unto a measure of age of the fullness of Christ" (Eph 4:13).

But there is contained within the Mystery of the incorporation of men with Christ in the unity of his mystical body an obstacle, two-fold in nature, preventing, or at worst, delaying the parousia of Antichrist. In Christ's last discourse to his disciples we begin to see the other (eschatological) side of the coin. On the one side, his disciples were invited to sprout like a mustard seed, develop-

---

[1]Fr. Fernand Prat, *Theology of St. Paul*, Vol 1, pp. 92-93.

ing into a tree capable of holding the birds of the air (all of mankind). This is in keeping with the exalted nature of the Church whose keys were not symbolic gifts and whose kingdom excluded none. This relationship between the Mystical Body of Christ and its head holds the key to the Book of Revelation. In that relationship the nature of the obstacle to the parousia of Anti-Christ was to be decided. For, it was not the developing Church that needed to be concerned about the appearance of Anti-Christ. In fact, it was within the Church's sufficient growth rate in Christ to develop into a permanent obstacle to the emergence of Anti-Christ and his conditionally projected short but cataclysmic intrusion into the "millennial" period of Church unity. It would all depend on Catholicism's accountability to grace in its Gospel calling. That is the other side of the coin, typified so graphically (as a deterrent to the future Church) in the Book of Revelation.

Our Lord's last discourse became a source of chronological confusion to the early Christians. St. Paul seems to have been aware of the signs preceding the Parousia, or second coming of Christ. Doomsday prophets, perhaps influenced mainly by his premature anticipation of the Parousia, were already writing their own epistles which terrified many of the faithful with details of the Last Judgment. It becomes a question as to how St. Paul could have mistaken the sign which would shortly precede the second coming of Christ, as though it (the sign) was about to be fulfilled. Earlier he had revealed the nature of that sign to his followers (but lost to us), when he described to them the *obstacle* delaying Anti-Christ's parousia, or coming. It is suggested here that the meaning of that *obstacle* to the coming of Anti-Christ finds its explanation in St. Paul's miscalculation of the extent to which the Gospel had already spread, and had been fervently received throughout the known world. We deduce from this that before Anti-Christ could appear, the "sound" of the Gospel should first go forth into all the earth. This being so, St. Paul's enthusiasm is to be blamed for his miscalculation: "But I say: Have they not heard? Yes, verily, their sound hath gone forth into all the earth, and their words unto the ends of the whole world" (Rom 10:18).

In short, Anti-Christ could not come until the Gospel had been preached to all nations. That was his obstacle...a simple obstacle of time. So simple is this explanation of the "obstacle" that it is easy to see why it wasn't recorded in Scripture. But why then did not St. Paul likewise anticipate this "man of sin" to appear presently on the scene? Because he was aware of the power of the Gospel over Satan; and he wrongly assumed this Gospel-potential for nullifying the rise of Anti-Christ was being realized. A sufficient growth-rate by the Mystical Body (the Church) in its mysterious union with its head, Christ, would, through the power of its Gospel (mustard seed) potential bring its own reward. It would bring unconditional victory over Satan by extending Anti-Christ's "obstacle" of *time* into a permanent obstacle.

St. Paul had not told the Thessalonians "after" the man of sin is revealed, as though his parousia was taken for granted. He left room for the non-materialization of the man of sin when he told them, "for unless there come a revolt, and the man of sin be revealed, the son of perdition" (2 Thes 2:3). His miscalculation then, no doubt pre-

cipitated by his eagerness to see Christ, was in misinter-
preting the phenomenal Christian growth-rate throughout the world (as a prelude to Christ's promised unity).
Consequently he anticipated an unconditional sanctuary
to follow shortly...a haven within which to gather all of
mankind (including last but not least, the Jews) into the
one fold of Christ: "Whom we preach, admonishing every man, and teaching every man in all wisdom, that we
may present every man perfect in Christ Jesus" (Col 1:28).
And so, casting aside any notion of a "revolt" during that
"millennial" period of reconciliation, he prematurely anticipated the Parousia of Christ.

Father Fernand Prat, S. J., seeing this two-fold nature
of the *obstacle* to Anti-Christ, is quite at a loss to explain it,
and little wonder:

"In one point only does Paul go beyond his
predecessors. He speaks of an obstacle which hin-
ders the immediate coming of Anti-Christ, and
gives us the following description of it: It is a person or something personified and at the same time
a physical or moral force. The obstacle is already
active and it checks the mystery of iniquity; it pre-
vents the advance of the wicked one. As soon as
this obstacle disappears, the field will be open to
Anti-Christ, whose appearance (parousia) seems
likely to precede but shortly the appearance
(parousia) of the Son of God. What is this obstacle? The Thessalonians had learned what it is
from the mouth of the Apostle, but we are ignorant of it now and everything leads us to suppose
that we shall always be ignorant of it."[2]

<hr>

[2]*Theology of St. Paul*, Vol. I p. 80.

If St. Paul told the Thessalonians the completed union of Christ as Head of his Mystical Body would have to precede Anti-Christ's parousia, then, whether Anti-Christ ever appeared on the scene, he could not hurdle such an obstacle. What interested Satan, however, was Christianity's accountability to the grace of its Gospel-calling (and hence, the penalty to Catholicism for compromising its Gospel-calling). It is in this sense that the freedom of choice on the part of Catholicism left the "millennial" Church vulnerable to Satan's plan against it. His insidious plans (mystery of iniquity) of exploiting man's materialistic propensity had to take into consideration that the gates of hell could never prevail over the Church, and that in spite of his efforts, a day would inevitably arrive when Gentile and Jew would become reconciled with one another in Christ, the Good Shepherd. His was not a plan of victory over the Church, therefore, but of revenge. It was a plan to victimize the Church's "millennial" haven—if only for one short but devastating "revolt" by "the man of sin."

As a sanctuary for the gathering of humankind into Christian unity in Christ, that "millennial" period of reconciliation would reflect the quality of Christianity's victory over Satan. Christianity's call (by means of a sufficient response to the grace of its calling) was to perfection: "even as your heavenly father is perfect." Otherwise its "unearned" entrance into the "millennial" haven of reconciliation would leave the sanctuary vulnerable to Satan's seeds of revolt. In spite of the idyllic "millennial" conditions of peace and harmony, the Church's compromised immunity against the seeds of revolt would not go undetected by some of the more discerning, and would eventually be exploited by one of them, the "man of sin." Notic-

ing the enthusiasm and spiritual naiveté of so many neophytes (of mass conversion), he would be aware of the van-
ity of the situation. And this would present a growing temptation for him to cast aside the fruits of reconciliation in
exchange for adulation by his own kind. Remembering that
even a greater revolt took place among the angels in heaven,
is it so hard to envision a revolt being divinely permitted
to take place during the period of Church unity in Christ?

"Let no man deceive you by any means, for
unless there come a revolt first, and the man of
sin be revealed, the son of perdition, who opposeth
and is lifted above all that is called God, or that is
worshiped, so that he sitteth in the temple of God,
showing himself as if he were God. Remember
you not that, when I was yet with you, I told you
these things? And now you know what
withholdeth, that he may be revealed in his time.
For the mystery of iniquity already worketh: only
that he who now holdeth do hold, until he be taken
out of the way. And then that wicked one shall be
revealed, whom the Lord Jesus shall kill with the
spirit of his mouth, and shall destroy with the
brightness of his coming, him whose coming is
according to the working of Satan, in all power
and signs and lying wonders." (2 Thes 2:3-9)

Before expanding on the rest of that passage, it must
be emphasized the key verse is 2 Thes 2:3: "for unless there
come a revolt, and the man of sin be revealed, the son of
perdition." Even though St. Paul paints a vivid picture of
the activities of Anti-Christ, in reality he is no more than
a harmless shadow within Satan's "mystery of iniquity," or
plan against the Church. Since a plan can be successful, or

it can fail, Anti-Christ could only emerge on one condition: through Christianity's insufficient response to its Gospel calling.

We see in 2 Thes 2:6, the *obstacle* is referred to as "what," and in verse 7, the obstacle is referred to as "who." Verse 6: "And now you know *what* withholdeth, that he may be revealed in his time." Verse 7: "For the mystery of iniquity already worketh; only that he who now holdeth, do hold, until he be taken out of the way. And then that wicked one shall be revealed." In verse 6, the obstacle (what) signifies the Mystical Body of Christ (a physical and moral force) in the process of growing. Time is required for "*it*" (as a moral force) to attain *its* destined growth in Christ: "But doing the truth in charity we may in all things grow up in him who is the head, even Christ" (Eph 4:15).

But in verse 7, a second description of that obstacle indicates that "he" (a person) remains an obstacle until *he* (Christ) unites his Mystical Body, the Church, to himself as *its* Head: "That he might present to himself a glorious church, not having spot or wrinkle, or any such thing; but that it should be holy, and without blemish" (Eph 5:27). *What* is completed in time? The Mystical Body. *Who* completes it? Christ its head. This two-fold obstacle of a person: "he who now holdeth" and of a moral force, "what withholdeth" satisfies the definition of Father Prat. No Anti-Christ could antedate the completion of the Mystical Body in Christ. And only then could the wicked one be revealed (following Satan's period in chains).

It is easy to see how St. Paul could miscalculate the miraculous worldwide rate of growth the young Church was making. Could the time of Christ's victory be near at last? No clue would escape his vigilant watch for Christ.

Hence his momentary confusion about his parousia. He caused his followers to get so concerned about it that some of them quit working altogether. Christ's teachings on this subject could no longer linger in the back of his mind. The Church had started out (literally, in the Cenacle) a house afire. Thousands of Jews were converted by a few sermons. Gentiles were lavishly gifted with charismatic powers. At this rate would it be long before the world would embrace the Shepherd of souls? The time for reconciliation with the Lamb of God was approaching. The obstacle (of time) was ending. He began to sense the power of the Gospel. "First I give thanks to my God through Jesus Christ, for you all, because your faith is spoken of in the whole world" (Rom 1:8). "But I say: have they not heard? Yes, verily, their sound hath gone forth into all the earth, and their words unto the ends of the whole world" (Rom 10:18). With total victory (we notice no expectation of Anti-Christ) over Satan so near, little time would remain for warnings and indoctrinations. Let the "whole world" come to the eucharistic banquet, and let the Jews too begin to enter the New Jerusalem.

But most of St. Paul's listeners were anything but enthusiastic about the Parousia. They were beginning to focus on the Last Judgment. St. James didn't help allay their fears by telling them "the coming of the Lord is at hand... Behold the Judge standeth before the door" (Jas 5:8, 9). So it did not take St. Paul long to realize, after landing in jail another time or two, along with another assortment of setbacks, that there was enough opposition to the spreading of the Gospel to prevent this final victory over Satan for some time to come. He began to sense that the Church must first be given time to better form the Christ-like image. He already told his edgy followers in effect, to disregard the false impressions they had. Ignore the numerous counterfeit epistles, wild speculations and false predictions concerning the proximity of Judgment Day. "That you be not easily moved from your sense, nor be terrified by spirit, nor by word, nor by epistles, as sent from us, as if the day of the Lord were at hand" (2 Thes 2:2).

He exhorted them to "stand fast and hold the traditions" (14). They have nothing to fear since they are the "first fruits unto salvation, in sanctification of the spirit, and faith of the truth" (12). Already, in his first epistle to them, he had given them some down to earth advice that, those who would sleep, or who would be drunk in the night should always be wary that "the day should overtake you as a thief" (1 Thes 5:4). But, by urging them to stand fast and hold the traditions, he was letting them know that the day of the Lord would come in its own due time. He counseled them first of all to obey the Gospel and secondly not to be anxious about a severe Judge. If the Church members fulfilled their potential in Christ, there would be no severe Judge for them. "For God sent not his Son into the world, to judge the world, but that the world may be saved by him" (John 3:17). This lack of judgment indicates that an unconditional salvation of the world rested on the potential of the Mystical Body as a moral force against Satan. And this would be the final testimony of our election and the reward of our "perfection," or fidelity, namely, the absence of Anti-Christ and of his apocalyptic revolt.

St. Peter prematurely anticipated the parousia of Christ also, but he gives a slightly different approach. He wrote: "But the end of all is at hand. Be prudent therefore, and watch in prayers" (1 Pet 4:7). One of Christ's prophe-

cies found in the Gospel of Saint Matthew could have influenced him, especially in view of the new enlightenment
he had concerning the spiritual kingship of Christ. He
knew that Jerusalem would be destroyed by the Romans,
who were even then building up their forces—but he now
had the added insight that the Jews would receive the
Gospel of Christ in the end. "And when they shall perse-
cute you in this city, flee into another. Amen, I say to you,
you shall not finish all the cities of Israel, till the Son of
man come" (Matt 10:23). As soon as he began to experience serious persecutions in Israel, it was logical to com-
bine all these signs into the one conclusion that the prophecy of Christ signified his second coming, and that it was
about to be fulfilled during his (St. Peter's) life-time. He
assumed that the destruction of Jerusalem would automatically melt the adamant resistance of the Jews toward Christ.
That anticipated conversion of course, was for him the
unmistakable sign of Christ's second coming.

VI

JEWISH GUILT AND PUNISHMENT: AN APOCALYPTIC GRACE

Today we all smile indulgently at the indiscretions of Adam and Eve for their aborted intermediary mission to posterity during an interrupted stay in the Garden of Eden. But if they were alive today, living, say, somewhere in upper New York, they probably wouldn't show themselves in public too often—judging by their likely steady inundation of hate mail and crank phone calls by an unforgiving segment of society. Take for example our Jewish brethren in today's world who still share that feeling of rejection. Witness a callous and unforgiving Christian segment of society forever castigating them for the fall from grace by the House of Israel's follow-up compromised intermediary Messianic calling to mankind. All of this simmering bias, mind you, in spite of St. Paul's directives to the early Christians against giving vent to such an arrogant presumption of righteousness. "Thou wilt say then: The branches were broken off, that I might be grafted in. Well: because of unbelief they were broken off. But thou standest by faith: be not high-minded, but fear. For if God hath not spared the natural branches, fear lest perhaps also he spare not thee. See then the goodness and the severity of God: toward them indeed that are fallen, the severity; but toward thee, the goodness of God, if thou abide in goodness, otherwise thou also shalt be cut off" (Rom 11:19-22).

Not that the whole Church founded on Peter can ever fail—-having been secured by so many divine promises in

holy writ—but, that each person in particular may fall. Over
and above this, however, St. Paul's warning to individual
members of the Church lends the passage to a deeper
eschatological interpretation. More succinctly, for the
maintaining of the Church's traditional intermediary mustard seed Gospel potential for mankind's direct and unconditional unification in Christ, it was incumbent upon
her members' sufficient collective cooperation with grace
so as to present an authentic Christian image within the
developing Mystical Body of Christ.

Thus, to probe deeper into St. Paul's warning to the
early Christians, it would seem that all three successive
intermediary participants in salvation history, Adam, the
House of Israel and the Catholic Church had a potential
for being "cut off." But how cut off? As in the cases of
Adam and the House of Israel we see they were cut off in
a punitive fashion within the framework of their intermediary callings to mankind, but not within the framework
of their final election in salvation history. This means that
the final end of their intermediary callings was providentially assured even though the providential means for fulfilling their calling were conditioned upon the sufficient
exercise of their intermediary prerogative: either directly,
and unconditionally, or punitively and by means of an alternate follow-up intermediary agency. Of necessity, intermediary callings to mankind (tests of obedience) entail
an element of conditionality. Jewish tradition held that the
Law was given to Moses as a mediator by means of angels.
"Now a mediator is not of one: but God is one" (Gal 3:20).

"Though this verse might mean that the Law
is inferior to the Promise because it comes from

God indirectly whilst the Promise comes without intermediary, St, Paul probably means that the Mosaic covenant was a bilateral alliance involving a mediator (Moses) and the possibility of the covenant failing through the transgressions of the Jews, whereas God's promise was unilateral, unconditional and indefectible and could not be modified by the Law."[1]

Father Prat S.J. explains further:

"But the presence of a mediator presupposes two contracting parties; and the act which results therefrom is a bilateral contract, producing on both sides rights and duties, the stability of which is conditional, since it can be canceled by common consent, or annulled through violation of it by one of the contracting parties. Very different will be the promise. Here God alone is concerned, and there is in him no fear of inconstancy, forgetfulness, or unfaithfulness. He binds himself by an oath in order to inspire man with more confidence. His promise is not dependent on the consent or the merit of anyone; and, as it is absolute and free of all conditions, it will not be repented of."[2]

This scenario likewise applies to Catholicism's follow-up intermediary Gospel calling to mankind in salvation history. Even though the intermediate ends of Israel's Mosaic prerogative for finding Christ and Christianity's Gospel prerogative for sufficiently "putting on Christ" (and

---

[1] A *Catholic Commentary on Holy Scripture*. p. 1117, 896g.
[2] Fr. Fernand Prat, *Theology of Saint Paul*, p. 184.

thereby giving the Church an efficacious Christian image) were not identical, their responsibility for developing a proper (humble) disposition was identical and could only be attained through their sufficient cooperation with the grace of their calling. For a third and final time the world's direct and unconditional fate hung in the balance...this time on the Church's intermediary Gospel prerogative of faith. By way of analogy, when the House of Israel came face to face with its promised Messiah, the appointed time arrived for him to throw the cup of gasoline (his Gospel message) on the log of Israel's Mosaic test of faith. Had Israel but become properly disposed through a sufficient response to the grace of her Messianic prerogative, or rather, as it were, through the heating and drying process of the chosen people's Mosaic calling, she would have become immediately graced by the unconditional gift of Christ's Gospel presence.

A faithful Israel would have ridden the wave of her meritorious disposition into the New Jerusalem, the Kingdom of Heaven, the Church. There would then follow the unfinished business for these new residents of Christ's Messianic reign: charismatically to "put on Christ," take up his Gospel in heroic fashion and systematically radiate the Church's intermediary prerogative for attracting mankind directly into the one fold of their divine Savior. Obviously, under these ideal conditions, Christ would not require that his harvesters bear the shameful cross from which he himself would have been spared by their belief in him. He had never even hinted that his followers bear anything more than his "sweet yoke and light burden" (Matt 11:30), and that they come to him for refreshment. Furthermore, there would have been no reason for him not to proclaim the cross at the very outset of his public life, were it not that he had to await the arrival of the "acceptable time" of the Temple leaders' formal decision for its determination. And lest we forget, the shedding of one drop of his blood in obedience to his Father's will would have sufficed. And so, it would happen that a heroic effort by these newly regenerated "Christians" aided immensely by the fruits of the Holy Spirit ("Be ye perfect as your Heavenly Father is perfect") would progressively transform the Church's universal image into an efficacious image of Christ, so essential to its intermediary Gospel prerogative over Satan's direct and unconditional defeat.

The significance of an unconditional triumph over Satan by the Church's Gospel mission to the world, in through and by Christ is pivotal. As just stated, the House of Israel's sufficient response to the grace of its Mosaic prerogative for entering its people directly and unconditionally into "the Israel of God" (Gal 6:16), which is to say, into the Church's mission of Christian unity, would have obviated two potential scenarios: the crucifixion of the Messiah, and as a consequence, a follow-up intermediary test of faith, namely, the intermediary Gospel test inherited by the Gentiles.

Ironically, in view of Israel's predestined final Messianic incorporation, Christ painted the loss of her compromised Mosaic prerogative for finding him directly and unconditionally, in apocalyptic "end of the world" language. "Amen I say to you, that this generation shall not pass, till all these things be done" (Matt 24:34). Precisely because of her final Messianic election the definitive loss of her intermediary role in salvation history took on the drastic proportions of apocalypse. As a result, her role was substituted for by an alternate providential means of grace—an alternate *modus operandi*—the Gentiles—for incorporating the world, as well as herself, into Christ's Mystical Body. And so, in essence, as a painful consequence of Israel's compromised Messianic prerogative, God stripped her of her pedagogue—the weak Law of Moses, given to her essentially to arouse in her a sense of sinfulness and penitence so necessary during her Mosaic test of faith. In a sense, God replaced the Law of Moses with yet another soul-searching pedagogue for her: the imperfect Gentiles themselves via the Church's follow-up Gospel test of faith in salvation history.

+ + + + +

In his concern to mitigate the nagging question of Jewish guilt and punishment, and to preserve Jewish Identity and Election in the process, Father Elias, O.C.D. would attempt to reverse the Church's intermediary role from the Gentiles back to the Jews (Hebrew Catholics) during the coming days of the Church's destined kerigmatic Gospel triumph in Christ over Satan. We quote three passages from his book, *Jewish Identity*, (Miriam Press, New York, 1987), pp 128-130:

"In the Epistle to the Romans, Chapter 11, St. Paul offers us another clue: 'Since their rejection meant the reconciliation of the world, do you know what their admission would mean? Nothing less than a resurrection from the dead.' St.

Paul is enlarging on what he had written in Rom 11:12: 'But if their transgression and their diminishing have meant riches for the Gentile world, how much more their full number!' We conclude, therefore, that the expression ¡resurrection from the dead" refers in the first place to the Gentiles. St. Paul is saying, perhaps in a veiled manner, that the Gentiles will one day abandon the faith he had offered them and die spiritually. The admission of the Jews would signal their resurrection."

"In Rom 11:19-23, St. Paul adumbrates the coincidence in time of the admission of the Jews and the apostasy of the Gentiles. In addressing himself to his Gentile neophytes, in an attempt to soften their arrogant attitude toward Jews, he develops his famous image of the olive tree and the branches: 'You will say, "Branches were cut off because of unbelief and you are there because of faith. Do not be haughty on that account, but fearful. If God did not spare the natural branches, he will certainly not spare you. Consider the kindness and the severity of God—severity toward those who fell, kindness toward you, provided you remain in his kindness: If you do not, you too will be cut off. And if the Jews do not remain in their unbelief they will be grafted back on, for God is able to do this.'" (p. 129)

"We are indebted to Lemann for the definition of the Biblical expression "apostasy of the Gentiles." It does not mean that all Gentile Christians will lose their faith, even to confine oneself to Europe. That there are still flourishing communities of Christians in Europe is in no way proof that the apostasy of the Gentiles has not taken place. The apostasy of the Gentiles is synonymous with the collapse of Christendom, not with the disappearance of Christianity. Our question was: When, according to Scripture, is the accession of the Jews due to occur? Our answer is that it will take place simultaneously with the apostasy of the Gentiles." (p. 130)

First of all, in reply to the above quotes of Father Elias, O.C.D., the Jewish convert is invited by the Church along with all Christians, to "put on Christ" by becoming assimilated into, or absorbed by the Son of David himself—who could never lose his Jewish identity—and ultimately become transformed by him into a "new creature" (2 Cor 5:17). And secondly, both their Jewishness along with that of all Jewry has been preserved by divine design simply by the fact alone that they are a people destined by election for conversion en masse into the waiting arms of their rightful Messiah. To what other people has God addressed such loving words as, "If I forget thee, O Jerusalem, let my right hand wither!" As for the bitter pill of Jewish punishment—how it pales during these promising signs of mankind's destined Christocentric integration into Christ's completed Body, the Church.

Once Christ aborted Israel's Mosaic prerogative for attaining a direct and unconditional Gospel adherence, however, the Jews could never succeed in circumventing the stigma of their apostasy in spite of their predilection, by being re-instated in the follow-up intermediary Gospel test of faith that was never intended for them. The reason is that Israel's Mosaic test of faith, although an end for recognizing Christ, was not an end in itself. Israel's Mosaic test of faith was her prerogative for entering directly and unconditionally into the Church's intermediary Gospel mission to mankind...in charismatic fashion. Comparing the Mosaic test of faith with the Gospel test of faith, therefore, is like comparing apples with oranges. Consequently, Israel's Gospel calling in, through and by Christ was to have been the Church's primary *modus operandi* for completing the Father's will in salvation history. What then shall we say about that lively eschatological language found in the Old Testament? Simply, that in view of Israel's promised final Messianic unification, her intermediary Gospel potential in, through and by Christ was the sole object of apocalyptic grace. In no way, therefore, could the Gentiles' follow-up intermediary Gospel test of faith be breached, or assumed, even by a remnant of Christian Hebrews. Ironically, this is true even to the extent of some possible large-scale apostasy within the body of the Church. It is impossible, however, that such an apostasy could parallel the House of Israel's Temple scenario. In other words, such a reversal would require the apostasy of Rome's Vicar of Christ, the Pope, along with his Magisterium!

It is only fitting, therefore, that two seemingly *non sequiter* approaches, one from the text of Saint Paul, the other from the lips of the dying Jesus should help shed light on the paradox involving Israel's negated theocratic role at the crucifixion of Christ. Saint Paul wrote: "Which none of the princes of this world knew, for if they had known it, they would never have crucified the Lord of glory" (I Cor 2:8). First of all, it must be pointed out that Israel's lack of knowledge stood between her and Christ's crucifixion. Put in another way, St, Paul's *if clause* pointed to the glaring possibility, which is to say, scenario in salvation history that would have precluded the total oblation of Christ's obedience to his Father's will "even unto death" for the redemption of mankind. As St. Thomas Aquinas says, "But that which is not impossible can be." He quotes Aristotle (Book 4 *Salvation*, 24:15): "In divinity being and possibility do not differ" (Aristotle *Physics* III, 4:203-30). For good reason, therefore, the Old Testament prophecies could never have limited Christ's redemptive act by etching his total immolation in stone. Such an immolation was not an essential ingredient for mankind's redemption. As St. Thomas has made it evident, "every action or suffering of His was salutary. For this reason Dionysius calls the human operation of Christ *theandric*, that is, 'God mannish'" Book 4: *Salvation*. And so we must look closely at Holy Scripture's employment of conditional prophecy and its intrinsic bearing (as a warning signal) on the Temple leaders even as they deliberated the taking of Christ's life.

In very fact, Christ dramatically reminded them shortly prior to their fatal decision, that the story of Nineveh's repentance at the preaching of Jonah was yet viable to the House of Israel as a type of its immediate Messianic fruition. Indeed, the Old Testament summed up very succinctly the two options open to Israel by a single equation, the Jonah equation: The repentance of Nineveh at the preaching of Jonah, as a type, or conditional prophecy foretelling Israel's sufficient Gospel response to the teaching of Christ...contrasted by Jonah's three days in the whale's belly, as a story which conditionally prophesied Christ's death and resurrection by way of a type that implied Israel's impenitence and insufficient Gospel response.

From the lips of the dying Savior on the Cross we get our first hint as to the complicated nature of Jewish guilt and punishment: "Father, forgive them for they know not what they do" (Luke 23:34). The only logic we might derive by comparing this passage with that of St. Paul quoted above is that Israel's sin consisted in not knowing. "Which none of the princes of this world knew; for if they had known it, they would never have crucified the Lord of glory" (I Cor 2:8). Technically, of course, they did not knowingly commit a sin of deicide since, as St. Paul stated, they never did know the divine Lord of glory. This did not prevent their neglect of the providential means at their disposal for discovering the Lord of glory, however, from becoming the spiritual impediment most responsible for breaking the heart of their Savior—which he so humanly lamented when he openly wept over his beloved City, "Jerusalem, Jerusalem, thou that killest the prophets, and stonest them that are sent unto thee, how often would I have gathered together thy children as the hen doth gather her chickens under her wings, and thou wouldst not?" (Matt 23:37).

Patently, though not a few of Israel's children were disposed to settle under the wings of their Lord and King, her spiritually defunct leaders, the "princes of this world," through the centuries had been systematically undermining the House of Israel's theocratic status. For, Israel alone had been providentially graced with the theocratic respon-

sibility of entering God's Chosen people directly and unconditionally into the Church's Gospel mission of
unity..."and thou wouldst not." Her compromise narrowed
down to the cataclysmic loss of a prerogative. Perhaps the
final straw for her princes of this world was their suppression of the very instincts within their souls which were
providentially prodded by the Old Testament's apocalyptic language. It was a language that only the foreknowledge of a Just and Merciful God could have revealed by
way of a warning to them not to compromise the intermediary fruition of their Mosaic calling.

Taken in this vein, Christ's dying words on the cross
for them might thus be expanded: Father, thy people need
forgiveness. Forgive them for having failed to learn of me
that I am meek and humble of heart. By election they remain thy chosen people, even though thou deny them the
continued pedagogic assistance of the Mosaic Law, which
had been given to inspire in them a humble longing for
redemption and an awareness of their spiritual inadequacy.
And so, thou dost temporarily cut them off, subjecting the
pathway of their final Messianic incorporation into the
pilgrim Church by means of a follow-up intermediary Gospel test of faith:...a test to the Gentiles, that, whether directly or by the grace of an apocalyptic intervention, will
succeed: "and they will hear it" (Acts 28:28).

Again, I say, forgive and heal them Father through
thy punitive cleansing grace during their apocalyptic period of exile, by stirring-up within their troubled souls a
gradual affinity to my Mystical Body, the Church, once it
begins to radiate in convincing fashion the divine light of
my authentic image. Forgive them, Father, for in thy Light,
they will see light. "For the wrath of God is revealed from

heaven against all ungodliness and injustice of those men that detain the truth of God in injustice: Because that which is known of God is manifested in them. For God hath manifested it unto them" (Rom 1:18,19).

PART TWO

The Apocalypse of It All

"We entreat you

not to receive

the grace of God

in vain."

(2 Corinthians 6:1)

I

A Concession

We must open the commentary by taking a peek at the back of the Book of Revelation. How many of us have first taken a sneak look at the ending of a detective novel before opening the first page!

"And I saw an angel coming down from heaven, having the key of the bottomless pit, and a great chain in his hand. And he laid hold on the dragon, the old serpent, which is the devil and Satan, and bound him for a thousand years. And he cast him into the bottomless pit, and shut him up, and set a seal upon him, that he should no more seduce the nations, till the thousand years be finished. And after that, he must be loosed a little time" (Apoc 20:1-3).

Heaven was meant to be Lucifer's "millennium," or mystical number of one thousand which represents eternity. But when he fell from grace, an angel laid hold on him and set him in chains for a thousand years, or eternity, interrupted for a brief period during which time he is given permission to plot against men and to release his fury upon them. That is to say, his chains were loosed "a little time." St. John used the vision of Satan's fall to cleverly disguise the Roman situation. By reversing the stages of Satan's fall, he was able to reveal the stages of Rome's fall from power. The first stage therefore of Rome's fall (verse 3) would entail the unchaining of a diabolical fury upon Christians for "a little time." Christianity failing to apostatize, Rome would be defeated (bound for a thousand years, verse 2).

By the same token, Christianity would enjoy such new-found freedom (due to Satan's mitigated power) that the whole Christian era would be likened to a millennium (1000 years! Forever!) But St. John had no way of knowing that his vision of Satan's unchaining was also a "type" of the Church's shortened (or interrupted) messianic reign. Should Catholicism fail to fulfill the Church's mustard seed potential for leading the world directly into a permanent messianic reign, then the world's entrance into the millennium (1000 days?), or indoctrination period of reconciliation of Jews and Gentiles in Christ, would be providentially stimulated through fear (by way of a divine concession to the Church) during which time Satan would be temporarily chained. And after an unspecified time "he must be loosed a little time"...which is to say, there would come a revolt and the "man of sin" would be revealed.

II

Spiritual Martyrs to the Harvest

Verse 4 of Apocalypse 20 continues: "And I saw seats; and they sat upon them, and judgment was given unto them; and the souls of them that were beheaded for the testimony of Jesus, and for the word of God, and who had not adored the beast nor his image, nor received his character on their foreheads, or in their hands; and they lived and reigned with Christ a thousand years."

The general interpretation is that those who "sat upon" the seats are to be the souls of the martyrs and saints living and reigning with Christ in heaven in the "first resurrection," which is that of the soul to the life of glory. But they could hardly come back and reign on earth during the "millennium" without the "second resurrection" of their bodies. "Blessed and holy is he that hath part in the first resurrection. In these the second death hath no power; but they shall be priests of God and of Christ; and shall reign with him a thousand years" (Apoc 20:6). And so, the saints of the "first resurrection" if taken in a wider sense of the spiritually martyred, would be for the most part, the elect, blessed with teaching credentials in the providential mission of Church unity that is to be completed during the millennium. Their resurrection would be to "election" or immunity from the second death, apostasy. On their heads would be martyr's crowns for having survived the spiritual martyrdom endured within the Church during Marxism's rape of mankind. In spirit they would share the Thrones of Judgment along with the martyrs in heaven associated with Christ in passing verdict on the world.

This type of spiritual martyrdom suggests the persevering grace of kingship and priesthood. These patient souls, then, are not only the martyrs or confessors already in heaven, but "all who do not worship the Beast, even though yet unborn" (i.e., the militant opponents of antichrist). "In your patience you shall possess your souls" (Luke 21:19). It would be their immediate good pleasure, as a sign of their "new life," to radiate an aura of evangelical magnetism and fervor during the "thousand years." There are many "living martyrs" of the faith being spiritually beheaded, especially the millions, some of whom were partially and others wholly freed at the dissolving of the Iron curtain. Pope Paul VI described this degree of faith in his audience, June 25, 1975: "The faith demands a profession, it demands a logic of thought and of life, it demands concrete consistency.

It involves, therefore, a transfer from the mind to the will, it involves a testimony, an effort, a resistance, a sacrifice, a `martyrdom,' as so many Christian generations, so many heroes of the faith have taught us." These "martyrs" will have been the ones who have "borne the burdens of the day and the heats" (Matt 20:12), who maintained traditional spirituality and the science of the saints, who remained with the Lamb, enduring a spiritual martyrdom in defense of the "word of God." "These shall fight with the Lamb, and the Lamb shall overcome them, because He is Lord of lords, and King of kings, and they that are with Him are called, and elect, and faithful" (Apoc 17:14). They will be the martyrs who "keep the commandment without spot, blameless, unto the coming of our Lord Jesus Christ" (1 Tim 6:14). "Here is the patience of the saints, who keep the commandments of God and the faith of Jesus" (Apoc 14:12).

III

First Beast: "The World"

Continuing Apocalypse 20, we see that these spiritual martyrs of the word of God, "had not adored the beast" (v.4). This beast is described more fully in Apoc 13:1: "And I saw a beast coming up out of the sea, having seven heads and ten horns, and upon his horns ten diadems, and upon his heads names of blasphemy." This First Beast with seven heads and ten horns, according to some commentators alludes to the whole company of infidels, enemies and persecutors of the people of God, from the beginning to the end of the world. Perhaps the First Beast is more importantly, a contributing factor to all those enemies of the people of God. In other words, this beast could be representing "the World" which dwells in the infamous triumvirate of "the World, the Flesh and the Devil." The seven heads, then, would be the seven Capital Sins, and the ten horns would be the Ten Commandments, which when the seven heads caused them to be violated, put, so to speak, feathers in the beast's cap, or as the Apocalypse describes it, diadems upon his horns. Each Capital Sin is capable of fomenting blasphemy (or persecution) against Christ, the Head of the Church.

Verse 3 of the 13th chapter hints at the First Beast's source of hidden power: "And I saw one of his heads as it were slain to death: and his death's wound was healed." This describes the chief Capital Sin: pride. When Satan (the dragon) was cast out of Heaven his pride was completely crushed. But from his exalted position in Heaven he was cast onto the earth and given a certain amount of power to do evil against the kingdom of Heaven, the Church, as we see in Apoc 12:4: "And his tail drew the third part of the stars of heaven, and cast them to the earth: and the dragon stood before the woman who was ready to be delivered: that, when she should be delivered, he might devour her son." Thus Satan, through the First Beast, was permitted to exercise his vindictiveness. In this sense his pride was revived, or "healed."

Apoc 13 continues, "And all the earth was in admiration after the beast. And they adored the dragon, which gave power to the beast: and they adored the beast, saying: Who is like to the beast, and who shall be able to fight with him? And there was given to him a mouth speaking great things, and blasphemies: and power was given to him to do two and forty months." This seemingly self-contained power that "the World" contains by which to allure the strong and sway the wills of the weak, is supplied by the "power of darkness," Satan. It is all part of the master strategy, embracing man's weakened spiritual and physical nature, and the exploitation thereof. Many who should know better, would grow to love worldly wisdom (especially from the mouths of anti-Christs "speaking great things"), and some would even come to the blasphemy (persecution) of Christ. "Saul, Saul, why persecutest thou Me?" (Acts 9:4)

This First Beast would erode the Jewish commitment to their Mosaic test of faith. Later on he would allure Christians as far as possible away from their commitment to their Savior's Gospel test. And their worldliness would unwittingly keep Satan's strategy viable through the centuries. Concerning "the World's" power for 42 months, see below, section XV under Magic Wand.

The next three verses of Apoc 13:6-8, describe the Man of Sin, or Anti-Christ, and will be enlarged upon later. However, we see here the general strategy of the dragon in the use of the first Beast, "the World," through the agency of Capital Sins and the breaking of the Ten Commandments. He would attempt to diminish the purity of intention of the faithful (through sin and corruption) to such a degree as to compromise the Church's unconditional potential for attracting the world directly to Christ. He knew the quick potential of the Church (along with Mary) to crush him: "And the God of peace crush Satan under your feet speedily" (Rom 16:20). So it was the function of the first Beast to weaken the tabernacle (Church) from within. With increasing blasphemy (persecution) the Church would be assaulted from without. In this way poverty, ignorance and confusion would be perpetuated sufficiently until circumstances "ripened" for the appearance of the second Beast.

IV

SECOND BEAST: A MAN FROM GORI

Apoc 13:11, introduces a second Beast coming up out of the earth: "And I saw another beast coming up out of the earth, and he had two horns, like a lamb, and he spoke as a dragon." Far be it that any man should fit this description, and yet a man is indicated (by way of a conditional prophecy), and Joseph Stalin makes a likely candidate.

Two horns would be part of his arsenal with which to butt the Church: Corruption and World Poverty. (Remember his famous quip: "How many divisions does the pope have?") These two horns would loom heavy in Satan's strategy. They are as "twin horns;" for corruption seeds poverty, and poverty spawns corruption. Corruption (especially when it worms its way into the hearts of consecrated men of God, and Church leaders) sponsors the world-wide poverty upon which the Communism (of the second Beast) most readily spreads.

Joseph Stalin was far from being a lamb, but he was "like a lamb," in that the second Beast will be named (19:20) the "False Prophet," which reminds us at once of our Lord's warning about "false prophets who come to you in sheep's clothing but inwardly are ravening wolves" (Matt 7:15). "Even after his death there would be perpetuated a vague subservient 'religion' which the State could patronize without damage to itself. This lingering role [of the second Beast, ed.] has managed to maintain its subtle mystique. He was no intellectual, though cunning enough. He was short, stocky, black-haired, ruffianly, with one arm longer than the other, his swarthy face being scarred by smallpox contracted in infancy. His Georgian accent gave his Russian speech a guttural [dragon-like, ed.] effect. One special brilliance flashed through: It was narrowly specialized and confined within the single crucial area of creative political manipulation. Outside the realm of pioneering political maneuver, in which Stalin's flair remains unsurpassed, his qualities appear in no way superhuman, apart perhaps from the dogged persistence with which he was accustomed to pursue to the death both his manifold goals and his innumerable enemies."[1]

Getting back to Apoc 20:4, we see that the second Beast caused the earth (except for the servants of God) to adore the first Beast and his image. This is in reference to Apoc 13:12: "And he executed all the power of the former beast in his sight; and he caused the earth, and them that dwell therein, to adore the first Beast, whose wound to death was healed." Stalin was the chief architect of Soviet totalitarianism. By destroying the remnants of individual freedom he promoted the godless state. This state ostensibly provides for all material security and self-sufficiency. To any self-deluded puppet there is not much beyond "the World" worth considering. In this way the first Beast is adored (to the exclusion, or crowding out of God).

But what about the image of the first Beast? What does it mean to adore not only the first Beast, but the image of the first Beast? Apoc 13:13 helps to clarify it. This verse (13) describes the powers of the second Beast, whom we suggest is Joseph Stalin. "And he did great signs, so

---

[1] *The New Encyclopaedia Britannica.* "Joseph Stalin," p. 579.

that he made also fire to come down from heaven unto the earth in the sight of men."

Now we begin to see the beast in the man. "And he did great signs." The signs that Joseph Stalin exhibited, though horrendous, were hardly sorceries. On the contrary, they were monstrous acts of wholesale terrorism. In accordance with the overall strategy of Satan, Stalin released an unparalleled wave of terror, cruelty and criminality. In 1917 he switched over from a moderate stand to the militant policy of the Bolsheviks who favored an armed seizure of power. This was to be his crossing of the Rubicon. When the *coup d'etat* occurred in October, he played an important role in wresting power from Russia's provisional government. Catholicism and Marxism were made mortal enemies in that instant. Is it a mere coincidence that his first official launching into a vicious, merciless life of cunning, mayhem and terror coincided, not only with the year or month, but it exploded on the scene within hours of Our Lady of Fatima's "miracle of the sun?" More than a coincidence, he prompted that spectacular display of divine intervention.

This occurrence was witnessed October 19, 1917 at Cova da Iria, Portugal, by 70,000 spectators who were attracted by a report that three children had been receiving visions of Our Lady. According to the testimony of the witnesses, the sun appeared on that wet and dismal day and seemed to tremble, rotate violently, and finally fall, dancing over the heads of the throng before it returned to normal. Did this "miracle" await until Stalin made his decision...or, as the Apocalypse puts it; "so that he (the second Beast, Stalin) made also fire to come down from heaven unto the earth in the sight of men" (13:13)? Did his great potential threat to the Church provoke the divine intervention of the "miracle of the sun"? Mary would show the Church the divine concern for its safety by her message to the three children and her "sign from heaven," described in Apoc 13:13 as "fire from heaven."

As for the tyranny ("great signs") of Stalin, they scarcely can be equaled. When his collectivization of farms in the Ukraine failed, "Stalin continued to export the grain stocks that a less cruel leader would have rushed to the famine-stricken areas. Some 10,000,000 peasants may have perished through his policies during these years." His purges provide another example of unmatched inhumanity "All other sections of the Soviet elite: the arts, the academic world, the legal and diplomatic professions—also lost a high proportion of victims, as did the population at large, to a semi-haphazard, galloping persecution that fed on extorted denunciations and confessions. These implicated even more victims until Stalin himself reduced the terror, though he never abandoned it. Stalin's political victims were numbered in tens of millions. His main motive was, presumably, to maximize his personal power."[2]

---

[2]Ibid., p. 578.

V

LEGEND OF THE GODLESS STATE

Apoc 13:14,15 connects the second Beast and "the image of the beast." "And he seduced them that dwell on the earth, for the signs, which were given him to do in the sight of the beast, saying to them that dwell on earth, that they should make the image of the beast, which had the wound by the sword, and lived. And it was given him to give life to the image of the beast, and that the image of the beast should speak."

The first thing that strikes one is that the second Beast (Joseph Stalin) did not have his own image made so that he himself would become apotheosized, or deified. Many tyrants attempt that. But Stalin viewed his process of deification with cynicism. He went along with it so that by his own seeming deification, he would give life to the image (godless utopia) the people made of the first Beast ("the World"). He would paint a materialistic utopia and hold it out to mankind as the ultimate goal of life. To help achieve this effect he would "speak" through that image by allowing the State to propagandize his attributes. "Stalin's biography was long obscured by a mendacious Soviet-propagated 'legend' exaggerating his prowess as a heroic Bolshevik boy-conspirator and faithful follower of Lenin,' the founder of the Soviet Union. In his prime, Stalin was hailed as a universal genius, as a 'shining sun,' or 'staff of life,' and also as a 'great teacher and friend' (especially of those communities he most savagely persecuted); once he was even publicly invoked as `Our Father' by a metropolitan of the Russian Orthodox Church. Achieving wide visual promotion through busts, statues, and icons of himself, the dictator became the object of a fanatical cult that, in private, he probably regarded with cynicism."[1]

The above amazing bit of history obviates a seeming contradiction to Stalin's incorporation into Apoc 13:14: "And he seduced them that dwell on the earth, for the signs which were given him to do in the sight of the beast." Frankly, how could any tyrant seduce those whom he has terrified? The answer, as the quotations above point out, is as intriguing as it is incredulous. This brings us back to the steel grip of Communism, where the "great signs" (or criminal acts of cruelty) of Stalin came to play their part. For he not only desired "the image of the first Beast" to be adored, but, tired of waiting for worldwide revolution (after the death of Lenin in 1924), he purged, plotted, executed and assassinated so as to promote "Socialism in one country." In this he portrays to the letter the words of Apoc 13:15,16: "that whosoever will not adore the image of the beast, should be slain. And he shall make all, both little and great, rich and poor, freemen and bondmen, to have a character in their right hand, or on their foreheads." What else does this describe but his police state? Stalin "failed to promote individual prosperity, yet he created a mighty military industrial complex and led the Soviet Union into the nuclear age."[2]

So far so good for the strategy of the Dragon! As for the "character in everyone's right hand," is it not the red

---

[1] *The New Encyclopedia Britannica*, p.576.
[2] Ibid., p.576

flag with the hammer and sickle? The "character on their foreheads," would symbolize hardcore Communism. For a variety of reasons the lesser indoctrinated and lesser militant would accept their enslaved condition. Some would wave the red flag for its having removed them from the extremes of poverty and "bourgeois corruption." Others, although not so desperate, would allow their material concerns to choke out their spiritual values by taking solace in the seductive promises of the hammer and sickle. Once swallowed up and controlled by Stalin's brand of Communism, the next generation would be given minor privileges, all due respect given to the image of the beast..."And that no man might buy or sell, but he that hath the character, or the name of the Beast, or the number of his name" (Apoc 13:17).

VI

666: What's in a Name?

What does this mean: "the name of the beast, or the number of his name?" The Apocalypse identifies the name of the man; for the numeral letters of his name make up the number 666. It has intrigued biblical experts and amateurs no end. Such names as Adolph Hitler, Julius Caesar...might fit the description. "Here is wisdom. He that hath understanding, let him count the number of the beast. For it is the number of a man: and the number of him is six hundred sixty-six" (Apoc 13:18).

St. John's "second beast" was most probably Nero, whose Latin name could be made to fit the numerical description 666. But Nero was the tyrant of his times, as the early Christians well knew. He did not produce the times; they produced him. As "the second beast," he had relevancy only to the early Church. He had no relevancy to the future Church save as a type of the Church's potential antagonist who, like himself, could only emerge under special circumstances. It all depended on Christianity's response to its Gospel test. It follows, therefore, that any future role of "the second beast" was conditional, and that if and when any individual should fill that role in the future, neither he nor his name was predicted in Holy Scripture. This means that only the times could produce a future "second beast" and not the other way around. Hence, Catholicism, by controlling the times could snuff out any future emergence of a "second beast."

As for the out-of-control times, doubtless they could produce any number of tyrants eligible to fulfill the conditionally prophesied role of a second beast, even if, or especially if they had to change their names to qualify as "the number of a man," 666. It is suggested here that Joseph Stalin fulfilled the conditionally prophesied role of the second beast. The original name of Stalin was Joseph Vissarionovich Dzhugashvili. He retained that name throughout his youth as well as in the seminary, where he secretly studied Marxist literature. But later, when he turned Bolshevist, and assumed editorship of the newly founded Bolshevist newspaper, Pravda, he was inspired (providentially, it would seem) to adopt the surname of Stalin, derived from the Russian word stal ("steel"), so that numerically his title (at least in today's near-universal English language) would change to 666: (Komrad?) Joseph Stalin.

VII

THE MILLENNIUM: A CLOSER LOOK

The spiritual "martyrs" of the Church Militant would harvest the world during the Church's promised millennial "chaining" of Satan just as surely as the bloody martyrs ushered the early Christians past Rome and into the primitive Church's millennial "partial chaining" of Satan. There seems, therefore, to be two "chainings" of Satan in his dealings with men. The first was a partial chaining of his diabolical power by Christ himself. No doubt Satan's crippled condition facilitated the primitive Church's saints and martyrs in their perseverance against his power of evil (Beasts) and persecution (Rome). As a result, these saints, and others "yet unborn" were "enthroned as priests of God", which is to say, graced to reign with Christ through their successors during the Church Militant's Christian (millennial) battle against a partially curtailed Dragon. St. John's main concern, however, was that some of his flock might weaken and apostatize or "die," so as not to have a "part in the first resurrection," which is to say, a part in the Church's first priestly victory over Babylon.

The purpose of a second millennium, or complete chaining of Satan following the final outcome of the Church's gospel mission to mankind only becomes apparent when we place in perspective Catholicism's special obligation during that mission. Obviously Satan is to be crushed and chained eternally, But whether he would be permitted to revive and inflict a "second death" upon a number of Christ's reconciled harvest would depend on how sufficiently Catholicism had utilized the Church's mustard seed prerogative over him. The "second death," therefore, was a real concern for the members of Christ's flock; but for Catholicism, this expression found in the pages of the Book of Revelation amounted to a conditional prophecy of Satan's "unchaining" and brief cataclysmic moment of revenge—cut short by the Parousia of Christ.

This "second" Christian millennium (during Satan's complete "chaining", which Apoc 20:3 describes in no uncertain terms), signifies, as the round number 1000 years suggests, an unspecified but perfect period of time. Yet, even though an angel is destined to seize Satan and thoroughly nullify his influence, "that he should deceive the nations no more," nevertheless, some of his power could be gradually mitigated beforehand so that the official millennium might be imperceptibly opened up after a lengthy period of time, into a thousand days "millennium," corresponding to the 1000 days of Christ's public life. For, the time leading (typally speaking) to Satan's "unchaining" cannot be anticipated as a thousand years, since the Parousia of Christ is to follow it "like a thief in the night."

To sum up then, the martyrs and saints, as suggested above, who reign with Christ in heaven "in the first resurrection," are to be taken (typally) to mean spiritual martyrs—such as the long-suffering souls most affected by the great Marxist experiment and its devastating aftermath—who will be resurrected (by "election") during the millennial period. As a result of their election, they will merit special consideration during the frightful endurance of Satan's final unchaining. Those days will be shortened so that the "second death" or apostasy will not be their lot. And, finally, "the rest of the dead" would be those who are dead in the sense that the Prodigal Son "was dead and is come to life again; he was lost, and is found" (Luke 15:32). Even the "dead," who have to be roused into their religious convictions however feeble, will be divinely prodded into the one true fold. This includes the likes of hardcore Communists themselves (with the "character on their foreheads") whose perverted escapades against God, and conscience can only be remedied by the divine "Potter" himself. Their degree of docility, and ultimate conversion to the word of Truth will thus be assisted (like that of the lesser obstinate) more by the spiritual loophole of a fear-induced awakening than by the "charity that casts out fear." It may take a great portion of that graduated "millennial" period of Christian utopia to move their souls. Not only will the Holy Spirit's inspired ecumenical warmth amaze them, but it will begin to melt Jewish resistance into following the Lamb of God.

All of these ecumenically groomed multitudes will have their robes miraculously turned white: " And one of the ancients answered, and said to me: 'These that are clothed in white robes, who are they? And whence came they?' And I said to him: 'My Lord, thou knowest.' And he said to me: 'These are they who are come out of great tribulation, and have washed their robes, and have made them white in the blood of the Lamb'." (Apoc 7:13,14).

VIII

Ecumenical Strays United

The "servants of God" were signed on their foreheads by the angels according to St. John's vision: "And I heard the number of them that were signed, an hundred forty-four thousand were signed of every tribe of the children of Israel" (Apoc 7:4) Who are the "elect," the "servants of God," the "signed?" Who are the ones whose names are written in the Book of Life?

The spiritual nature of Satan gives him a great power over the world and the laws of nature. The Apocalypse does not scratch the surface of the evil he could do if permitted by God. "And the Lord said. 'Simon, Simon, behold Satan hath desired to have you, that he may sift you as wheat:'" (Luke 22:31). What the Book of Revelation reveals (as a type) is the evil to which God will limit Satan under the ripest of circumstances. St. John would tell his flock that they had something to say about those circumstances.

The first three chapters of the Apocalypse not only expose the seeds of destruction but they reveal the secret of predilection. In plain language they show that the servants of God, the elect, the ones signed on their foreheads and with their names inscribed in the Book of Life didn't just happen. That these marks of predilection had to be merited is why St. John was commanded to write instructions and admonitions to the seven churches of Asia. Obviously there was hope of crushing Satan, for it would be futile to warn against an inevitable doom. Seven churches were singled out, which is a round number representing the Church as a whole. St. John praises the good they are doing, yet he cautions against certain predominant imperfections among them. However, each imperfection when wholeheartedly combated, brings its own individual mark of predilection to the servants of God. And only in this way would the Church speedily fulfill her mission of gathering the one fold under the one Shepherd. The Church must grow, and not without growing pains.

Trials seem to be a virtual necessity nudging us to apply the steady flow of graces into a mark of predilection. Our calling was for us to work together within and through the Church so that her mission of union with Christ as Head might be quickly accomplished for the benefit of all mankind. This would also help explain the perplexity found in the opening verses of the Apocalypse: "The Revelation of Jesus Christ, which God gave to him, to make known to his servants the things which must shortly come to pass:" (1:1). It is not world destruction that is predicted, but trials "...for the time is at hand" (1:3). The dooms, if they do come, could not come shortly, but must await the verdict of Christian accountability to the grace of its Gospel test.

To the bishop of the church at Ephesus St. John was told to write "And thou hast patience, and hast endured for My name, and hast not fainted. But I have somewhat against thee, because thou hast left thy first charity." (Apoc 2:3,4) This is an admonition to the Church as a whole to do penance for a tendency of compromising its mission, and to be constant in watching and praying. Persevering in this way is to "put on" a special mark of predilection: a living faith and a taste of divine wisdom: "To him that overcometh, I will give to eat of the tree of life, which is in the paradise of my God" (Apoc 2:7).

The second church at Smyrna suffered from poverty and from internal dissention from Jewish converts still wishing to observe the legalisms of their former religion. This church was instructed to learn patience during persecutions and imprisonment, and attain the crown of life (spiritual martyrdom). "Fear none of those things which thou shalt suffer. Behold, the devil will cast some of you into prison that you may be tried, and you shall have tribulation ten days. Be thou faithful until death: and I will give thee the crown of life" (Apoc 2:10). The Church (typically speaking) is invited to suffer valiantly and thus accomplish her mission quickly ("ten days"). At any rate, this spiritual martyrdom brings with it the predilection of a gradual immunization from the spirit of apostasy. This will be the prerogative of the elect, should there come a millennial revolt. "He that shall overcome, shall not be hurt by the second death" (2:11).

To the church at Pergamus St. John was told to write: "But I have against thee a few things; because thou hast there them that hold the doctrine of Balaam, who taught Balac to cast a stumbling block before the children of Israel, to eat, and to commit fornication. So hast thou also them that hold the doctrine of the Nicolaites" (2:14,15). Like Balaam, the biblical prototype of religious compromise, the Nicolaites forfeited their Christian faith to paganism. The Church must resist this temptation toward secularism if it is to accomplish its mission to the world in the quickest possible time of "ten days"...(as a type of its direct and unconditional triumph over Satan). This accomplishment will be helped by yet another mark of predilection which is the spirit of renewal: "To him that overcometh, I will give the hidden manna, and will give him a white stone, and in the stone, a new name written, which no man knoweth, but he that receiveth it" (2:17). This rebirth in Christ is a predilection of victory and joy in Christ, and a "peace which surpasseth all understanding" (Phil 4:7).

The church at Thyatira exhibited much faith and charity; yet there was a marked inclination toward the World with its enticements and seductions of Jezebel. Most abominable of all are worldly prelates whose life-styles contradict the very nature of their calling. It is largely due to their indifference and impenitence that we owe the historical splits within the Church. The remedy for this abomination: Be conscientious about smaller regulations and the humdrum easy obligations. This docility will gain for one the predilection of sharing in Christ's messianic authority. "And he that shall overcome, and keep my works unto the end, I will give him power over the nations" (2:26). Such evangelic magnetism will be utilized by the elect during the millennial period of reconciliation.

The church at Sardis got a special reprimand too; "I know thy works, that thou hast the name of being alive: and thou are dead." "...For I find not thy works full before my God" (Apoc 3:1,2). Feverish activism can never substitute for a living faith. This especially fits the description of extremist "ecumenists." For example, not a few of them have pushed all sorts of abominable practices in the name of sexual liberation. "But thou hast a few names in Sardis, which have not defiled their garments; and they shall walk with me in white, because they are worthy. He that shall overcome, shall thus be clothed in white garments, and I will not blot out his name out of the book of life, and I will confess his name before My Father, and before His angels" (3:4,5).

As for the Philadelphians, if they have any fault, it is perhaps a timidity, or backwardness sometimes found amongst unlettered peasants. But to the church at Philadelphia was promised the greatest predilection of all, resulting from their incorporation in Christ. By enduring religious persecution in and for Christ, they preserved the doctrine of Christ's endurance; "Because thou hast kept the word of my patience, I will also keep thee from the hour of temptation, which shall come upon the whole world to try them that dwell upon the earth" (Apoc 3:10). Their chief persecutors were the Jews. The sheer evangelical beauty of their steadfast example will melt the hearts of these sophisticated tormentors so that they will "come and adore before thy feet" (3:9).

By using their "little strength" in the face of staggering odds, a door will be opened. They are promised the predilection of a new name in Christ, in the new Jerusalem, the Church. Being thus incorporated in Christ through the Church, they will in turn give Him a New Name: the Mystical Christ-Jesus. "He that shall overcome, I will make him a pillar in the temple of my God; and he shall go out no more; and I will write upon him the name of my God, and the name of the city of my God, the new Jerusalem, which cometh down out of heaven from my God, and my new name" (Apoc 3:12). "A little strength" therefore, is the antidote for timidity. "Because thou hast a little strength, and hast kept my word, and hast not denied my name" (3:8). How clear is this message which patently tells us that the Mystical Body of Christ was designed to conquer the world through a sufficient degree of docility on our part!

The church of the Laodiceans cuts itself off if for no other fault than a lackluster tepidity. Their negligence emphasizes the interdependence of predilection upon honest effort. They are told that even the wicked have greater claim to predilection than they: "But because thou art lukewarm, and neither cold, nor hot, I will begin to vomit thee out of my mouth" (Apoc 3:16). Not that Christ ever lacks tender intimacy for any of us. "Such as I love, I rebuke and chastise. Be zealous therefore and do penance. Behold, I stand at the gate, and knock. If any man shall hear my voice, and open to me the door, I will come in to him, and will sup with him, and he with me" (3:19,20).

So it is, the Church's mission hinges on a respectable degree of perseverance in the ways of virtue and growth in Christ by her members, as does our personal predilection and inscription into the Book of Life. This relationship between election and perseverance is summarized by St. Paul: "Therefore I endure all things for the sake of the elect, that they also may obtain the salvation, which is in Christ Jesus, with heavenly glory. A faithful saying: for if we be dead with Him, we shall live also with Him. If we suffer, we shall also reign with Him. If we deny Him, He will also deny us" (2 Tim 2:10,11).

IX

THE MASS:
A EUCHARISTIC RALLYING POINT

By comparing Apoc 20:6 with 7:17, we can envision an alternative to Christ's physical (animated) presence during the millennium. Apoc 20:6 seems to favor Christ's bodily presence: "But they shall be priests of God and of Christ; and shall reign with Him a thousand years." However, the fact that all those who reign with Christ are not only the servants of God but priests, identifies with the holy sacrifice of the Mass. There is no question of all the servants of God becoming ordained priests. More significantly, the sacrifice of the divine Victim is to be the central source of fervor during the millennium. And all the faithful who offer this Victim to the Father together with the invisible Christ and with the celebrant of the Mass truly share the priesthood of God and of Christ. This has always been a consoling teaching of the Catholic Church.

We find it reflected in Apoc 7:17: "For the Lamb, which is in the midst of the throne shall rule them, and shall lead them to the fountains of the waters of life, and God shall wipe away the tears from their eyes." For it strongly reminds us of Christ's promise: "But the water that I will give him, shall become in him a fountain of water, springing up into life everlasting" (John 4:14). It is this Eucharistic Lamb, therefore, that will be the rallying point of faith during the millennium.

X

AN INHERENT WEAKNESS

One tragic drawback about the wholesale conversion that will take place during the relatively short (numerically perfect) time of the millennial sanctuary is that the weakness of faith will be retained in many of the people. Even though they find themselves in a utopia where: "There shall be no more hunger, nor thirst, neither shall the sun fall on them, nor any heat" (7:16), nevertheless, it will remain incumbent upon them to live and grow in the virtues of faith, hope and charity.

The very fragility of faith detectable in so many of them—especially the ones lacking in vigilance—could provide the temptation for some discerning individual (Anti-Christ) to seduce them for his own vain dreams of grandeur. With the help of Satan (when loosed) he could flatter, charm and overwhelm an army of followers. This, in essence, is the pride-trap Lucifer himself fell into when he was once the brightest star above in the Utopia of utopias. But, to repeat, such a concession to Satan as this could only take place on the sole condition of Catholicism's gospel compromise of the Church's mustard seed prerogative over him.

XI

THE ANTI-CHRIST

This rambling tour of the Apocalypse can no longer avoid investigating the exclusive haunts of Anti-Christ. "Little children, it is the last hour; and as you have heard that Anti-Christ cometh, even now there are become many antichrists: whereby we know that it is the last hour" (1 John 2:18). The Man of Sin, or Anti-Christ, however, cannot be mistaken: "Let no man deceive you by any means, for unless there come a revolt first, and the man of sin be revealed, the son of perdition..." (2 Thes 2:3), We find the key to this double use of the term Antichrist in Apoc 13:5-8.

It involves the first beast with the seven heads (Capital sins). It will be recalled that the Dragon gave this beast his own strength: "and all the earth was in admiration after the beast" (13:3). This beast, we identified as "the world," which seemingly has its own built-in capacity to allure us. We see, however, in verses 5 and 6 two distinct references to this beast's mouth. Verse 5 refers to "antichrists": "And there was given to him a mouth speaking great things, and blasphemies: and power was given to him to do two-and-forty months" (Apoc 13:5). In verse 5, the beast is given a "mouth speaking" great things, and blasphemies, and power to corrupt, for a designated period of time (two and forty months). These antichrists were the forerunners of the Anti-Christ. Put in another way, they emanate from the "small mouth" of this beast, But verse 6 shows us the "big mouth," of the beast *opening up* (at the time of the great revolt). The beast's mouth which was given to it at first for lesser strikes against the Church, now *opens up* for Anti-Christ's all-out onslaught. "And he opened his mouth unto blasphemies against God, to blaspheme His name, and His tabernacle, and them that dwell in heaven" (13:6).

The Anti-Christ will be helped by the eighth beast which Apoc 17:8 personifies as the power of Satan: "The beast, which thou sawest, was and is not, and shall come up out of the bottomless pit, and go into destruction: and the inhabitants on the earth (whose names are not written in the book of life from the foundation of the world) shall wonder, seeing the beast that was, and is not." This power is Satan acting through the world (Capital Sins) and so thoroughly through the Anti-Christ as to make him appear to be the devil incarnate. The inhabitants of earth, who previously had wilfully and whimsically rejected the graces of God, will begin to wonder openly at the powers of wickedness. As a worker of marvels, the Anti-Christ will find it a simple matter to seduce many weaker souls, especially the scattered remnants formerly associated with the hard-core communists, recipients of the "character of the beast." In general, they are the many peoples who neglected their spiritual existence in an exaggerated concern about their material welfare, content to place their security in various shades of Socialism closely aligned to the Hammer and Sickle. It would only be natural for them to hanker after the "fleshpots of Egypt" and to daydream about former delights of Mammon.

XII

Perseverance (in one's calling): An Attitude of Predilection

The revolt will be devastating. Anti-Christ will prevail over everyone, if given enough time. But, for the sake of the elect, he will be cut short. "And it was given unto him to make war with the saints, and to overcome them. And power was given him over every tribe, and people, and tongue, and nation" (Apoc 13:7). In the next verse we get a peek at the ones who do finally submit to the Anti-Christ: those "whose names are not written in the Book of Life of the Lamb, which was slain from the beginning of the world" (13:8).

The mercy and grace of God from the beginning, was given in view of Christ's obedience (even unto immolation). If their names are not written in the Book of Life of the Lamb, verse 10 goes on to show that no one's name is written in that book who treats his obvious rule of life with impunity. Anyone can be saved at any time, but it is the change of attitude (towards God) that merits a person's name being inscribed in the Book of Life. The foreknowledge of God merely takes note of our final decision. Our changing to the correct attitude, of course, is no mere whim. Not to change it is to become vulnerable to Anti-Christ.

A correct attitude is developed through the basics of fear of God (the "beginning of wisdom"), simplicity and purity of heart. It nourishes the Catholic instinct. Verse

10 expresses this truth (in the form of a riddle) by giving two examples of morality that are obvious to all—with the exception of the perverse of heart. The riddle displays perversity as a self-induced blindness of the obvious: "He that shall lead into captivity, shall go into captivity: he that shall kill by the sword, must be killed by the sword" (13:10). The point is, no one becomes perverse overnight. That mentality, or attitude of impunity is first developed on the battlefields of the easy and the obvious. The habitual spurning of relatively easy and "insignificant" counsels of perfection is devastating to our spiritual progress.

The Sermon on the Mount is not really that complicated, but when glossed over, easily gets out of focus. That is why a winning attitude puts our names into God's Book, at least in invisible ink, until the magic powder of perseverance brings them out into bold relief: "Here is the patience and the faith of the saints" (13:10). "But the foundation God has laid stands firm. It bears this inscription: 'The Lord knows those who are his; and, 'Let everyone who professes the name of the Lord abandon evil'." The lesson is that if a person will but "cleanse himself of evil things, he may become a distinguished vessel, dedicated and useful to the master of the house and ready for every noble service" (2 Tim 2:19,21).

The vision of our Father's calling to predilection of the "little ones" filled Christ's humanity with joy in the Holy Spirit, not only because of their calling, but because of his intervening role. It would prompt him to exclaim to his apostles "Behold I have given you power to tread upon serpents and scorpions, and upon all the power of the enemy: and nothing shall hurt you. But yet rejoice not in this, that spirits are subject unto you; but rejoice in this that your names are written in heaven. In that same hour, he rejoiced in the Holy Ghost, and said: I confess to Thee, O Father, Lord of heaven and earth, because Thou hast hidden these things from the wise and prudent, and hast revealed them to little ones. Yes, Father, for so it hath seemed good in Thy sight" (Luke 10:19-21).

The little ones avoid the perversion that is justly condemned to eternal damnation. Ordinarily it is the steady and willful abuse of easier spiritual obligations that leads to perversion. Therefore, it is not our isolated grievous sins that justify damnation so much as it is this growing cancer of perversion. Perversion leads us little by little into those more serious lapses and consequently into a life of wickedness. "If any man have an ear, let him hear" (Apoc 13:9).

XIII

Mystery of Iniquity

Apocalypse 17 lifts a corner of the veil covering sin. It becomes evident that what seems to be raw uncontrolled sin is very much organized for a devious purpose. We get, in effect, a glimpse of the "Mystery of Iniquity." We find here, not only an insight into the nature of sin, but also the nature of Satan's punishment; for he had a dilemma. The very men he seduces or fails to seduce, will come back to haunt him, once he is thrown back forever into the bottomless pit. In the colorful language of the Apocalypse this dilemma is expressed by the personification of Satan's seductive powers, which is here depicted by the prophetess Jezebel. She was given time to "do penance." This is another way of saying that Satan had a choice to consider...and in spite of the consequences to himself, he chose the ways of "fornication." "And I gave her a time that she might do penance, and she will not repent of her fornication" (Apoc 2:21). Here, then, is Apocalypse 17:

1. And there came one of the seven angels, who had the seven vials and spoke with me, saying: Come, I will show thee the condemnation of the great Harlot, who sitteth upon many waters.

2. With whom the kings of the earth have committed fornication; and they who inhabit the earth, have been made drunk with the wine of her whoredom.

3. And he took me away in spirit into the desert. And I saw a woman sitting upon a scarlet colored beast, full of names of blasphemy, having seven heads and ten horns.

4. And the woman was clothed round about with purple and scarlet, and gilt with gold, and precious stones and pearls, having a golden cup in her hand, full of the abomination and filthiness of her fornication.

5. And on her forehead a name was written a mystery: Babylon the great, the mother of the fornications, and the abominations of the earth,

6. And I saw the woman drunk with the blood of the saints, and with the blood of martyrs of Jesus. And I wondered, when I had seen her, with great admiration.

7. And the angel said to me Why dost thou wonder? I will tell thee the mystery of the woman, and of the beast which carrieth her, which hath the seven heads and ten horns.

8. The beast, which thou sawest, was, and is not, and shall come up out of the bottomless pit, and go into destruction: and the inhabitants on the earth (whose names are not written in the book of life from the foundation of the world) shall wonder, seeing the beast that was, and is not.

9. And here is the understanding that hath wisdom. The seven heads are seven mountains, upon which the woman sitteth, and they are seven kings:

10. Five are fallen, one is, and the other is not yet come, and when he is come, he must remain a short time.

11. And the beast which was, and is not: the same also is the eighth, and is of the seven, and goeth into destruction.

12. And the ten horns which thou sawest, are ten kings, who have not yet received a kingdom, but shall receive power as kings one hour after the beast.

13. These have one design: and their strength and power they shall deliver to the beast.

14. These shall fight with the Lamb, and the Lamb shall overcome them, because he is Lord of lords, and King of kings, and they that are with him are called, and elect, and faithful.

15. And he said to me: The waters which thou sawest, where the harlot sitteth, are peoples, and nations, and tongues.

16. And the ten horns which thou sawest in the beast: these shall hate the harlot, and shall make her desolate and naked, and shall eat her flesh, and shall burn her with fire.

17. For God hath given into their hearts to do that which pleaseth him: that they give their kingdom to the beast, till the words of God be fulfilled.

18. And the woman which thou sawest, is the great city, which hath kingdom over the kings of the earth.

Commentary on *Apocalypse*, Chapter 17

Verse 3. The scarlet colored beast represents the World. The woman sitting upon the beast is the enchantment and seductive powers of the World. And on her forehead a name was written: a mystery. She is Jezebel, drunk with the blood of the saints, and with the blood of martyrs of Jesus. Those who reject the blandishments of the world must become fools for Christ's sake. This is easily explained by the words of Christ to his Apostles: "If you had been of the world, the world would love its own: but because you are not of the world, but I have chosen you out of the world, therefore the world hateth you" (John 15:19).

Verse 8. The beast "which was, and is not: the same also is the eighth and is of the seven." This beast is the hidden power of Satan in all seven beastly powers so much so that all seven (Capital Sins) together resemble one terrible eighth beast. Satan, therefore, is the power of sin in the World; he is the persuasiveness of Jezebel and the seductiveness of Babylon. He will captivate those unfaithful to their Gospel calling.

Verse 9. The power of Satan works in the World through the seven deadly sins. Yet each of the deadly sins receives his undivided attention as king.

Verses 10, 11. Just as the seven deadly sins represent the kings, or powers of Satan, so it is that five times divine Providence has eclipsed his power outright: (1) when, as prince of the angels, he was cast out of Heaven; (2) by the Immaculate Conception of Mary; (3) by the Virgin Birth; (4) by the Resurrection of Christ; (5) by the establishment of the Church of Christ. Nevertheless his power is still felt ("one is"), though Providence has partially checked it as a result of Christ's redemptive mission. And finally, "when he is to come" his seductive powers will be thoroughly checked when he is "chained" during the millennium. Any subsequent (or typal) unchaining would be brief, after which he would be crushed for all time.

Verses 12,13. Discusses the design of sin. Laws protect individuals and communities, but concupiscence ironically received greater potential over our weak human nature after the law of Moses was given. As St. Paul says: "But I do not know sin, but by the law; for I had not known concupiscence, if the law did not say: Thou shalt not covet. But sin taking occasion by the commandment, wrought in me all manner of concupiscence. For without the law sin was dead. And I lived some time without the law. But when the commandment came, sin revived, And I died. And the commandment that was ordained to life, the same was found to be unto death to me. For sin, taking occasion by the commandment, seduced me, and by it killed me" (Rom 7:7-11).

Although breaking the Ten Commandments brings death to individuals, it cannot destroy the Church. However, the efficiency of her mission is seriously affected by sin, for it compromises some of her prerogatives designed to attract the world to Christ. This is the area Satan is given in which to maneuver. Put in the language of the Apocalypse, these ten horns on the beast, that is to say, the breaking of the Commandments in general, form a powerless kingdom against the Church. Therefore, if these ten horns, or kings, are to reach their potential, their efforts must be centralized according to an evil design, or master plan, which Scripture calls the "mystery of iniquity."

Christ founded his Church on a rock, and the gates of hell would plan in vain to prevent the Church from fulfilling his promised mission to the world through it. Yet Satan saw a certain providential condition attached to the Christian mission of unity—and laid his plans accordingly. What he saw was a potential for "sin against the Ten Commandments," or "ten kings" to gain a "victory."

Catholicism had the freedom of two choices of procedure for fulfilling the Church's providentially blessed mission to mankind. One choice would be for Church leaders and members to cooperate sufficiently with the grace of their Gospel calling by "putting on the image of Christ" in the designated time. By this acceptable degree of docility the Church would gradually realize her potential for attracting the world unconditionally into a completed Mystical Body joined to Christ as Head. Sin could never overwhelm such a healthy union, and consequently, the "ten kings" would be prevented from gaining a "victory" (revolt of Antichrist) during the millennial period of reconciliation.

On the other hand, a Catholic insufficient cooperation with the grace (mustard seed potential) of its Gospel calling would directly reflect a poor "Christian" image. God could not force a Christ-like image upon the members of his chosen flock, even though he required that image to be essential to the unconditional conversion of the world. Christianity's failure itself, to take full advantage of the mustard seed potential would unleash the world's propensity for self-destruction. Sin constructs its own time bomb —its own Deluge, so to speak. This ironically plays into the hands of providence for acting as a prod towards mankind's reconciliation process in Christ.

This analogy of the Deluge is not a complete picture. The wicked who experienced the slowly rising waters of the Deluge were given this prod solely as a last merciful opportunity to examine their consciences and to exhume, so to speak, the futility of their long-suppressed lights and willful obstinacy. Their pending extinction, however, was a foregone conclusion. But the modern Deluge-like threats—from AIDS to genocide needs not deteriorate into an apocalypse of nuclear exchange. For that would nullify Christ's mission of defeating the works of Satan. Thus, in both of these extreme examples there is a prodding by God. So that in both cases of a world-wide chaotic self-inflicted deluge-like condition, His freely extended invitation for sinners to come to Him is solely dependent upon His initiative of mercy reaching out to them.

An opening was needed by Satan (the Beast which "was and is not") before he could introduce the Anti-Christ into the millennial unity, so as to extend the time of his power by a short-lived "victory" of revenge. His plan was to utilize this Christian vulnerability to the ten horns, "which are ten kings who have not yet received a kingdom." These "ten kings" we represent as sins against the Ten Commandments. According to Satan's hoped-for strategy, they would multiply into the Catholic "sin of omission," eroding the Christian duty of forming a salvific Christ-like image. Christians were duly warned against placing hay, wood or stubble on the Church's foundation. Not that their negligence could bring the Church under the heel of Satan—

for that in itself would constitute the gaining of a kingdom by the ten kings.

The chief function, therefore, of the "ten kings" would be to weaken the Christian purity of intention, and thereby dull the "Christian" image...an image so necessarily endowed with charisma for harvesting the fields "white already to harvest" (John 4:35). World corruption and world poverty would spread unhindered in direct proportion to this compromise of the gospel. They would present a plum for the picking. A new deceitful voice would begin to echo from the wilderness. A new mendacious gospel would begin to be preached from the housetops—the gospel according to Karl Marx. In the imagery of the four horsemen (Apoc 6:2-8), the rider on the white horse receives a bow and a crown, and goes forth to conquer. He is Satan himself receiving permission to extend Godless Power gradually through his choice cavalry of War (the red horse of aggressive imperialism),of Famine (the black horse of poverty), and of Death (the pale horse of decay and corruption).

The millennium would last "one hour after the beast" was chained. Up to this time, the elect would have had time to gather all men into the one fold under the one Eucharistic Shepherd. Many of these converts would become "faithful" during the period of reconciliation. Others would allow themselves to become easy prey to the Anti-Christ. Perhaps not a few of these latter would long to revert to their old glory days in the Communist regime. "Gog" could rise again, carrying aloft the banners of the ten kings. Here is where the "ten kings" receive their kingdom and power, as the revolt of Anti-Christ envelops the millennial utopia. But the "elect and faithful" (verse 14) would be helped by the Lamb and King of kings to overcome Satan and all his power.

In verse 15, we begin to see the true nature of sin as well as the nature of Satan's dilemma. The harlot is Jezebel with all the charms, enchantments, lures and seductiveness that the genius of Satan uses to mask from us the bitter fruits of sin and of compromised virtue. The peoples and nations and tongues who fell victim to Jezebel will not only hate her, but they will individually take comfort in the knowledge that their degree of seduction by Jezebel directly corresponds to Satan's added torments in the bottomless pit. Satan will not only feel a loss of the power and range that he enjoyed through "Jezebel," but he will be forced to drink her blood for all eternity—much in the way a wounded pig sucks back its draining blood. Satan will become the object of scorn and ridicule both of the just and unjust. The unjust will see that as bad off as they are, he will be much worse off—and one reason he will be worse off is because of his sin ("fornication") against them.

These ensnared violators of God's Commandments will curse and taunt him in proportion to their seduction by the harlot "Jezebel." Her influence was great indeed, "For thy merchants were the great men of the earth, for all nations have been deceived by thy enchantments. And in her was found the blood of prophets and saints, and of all that were slain upon the earth" (18:23,24). Was it not this seductive voice of Jezebel in Satan that once tempted Christ with a dazzling display of power and overwhelming enchantments: "...and he said to Him: to Thee will I give all this power, and the glory of them; for to me they are delivered, and to whom I will, I give them (Luke 4:6).

XIV

SEVEN TRUMPETS AND SEVEN VIALS

Apocalypse 8 deals with seven trumpets corresponding to the seven vials, or bowls found in Apoc 16, revealing from the vantage point of God's infinite foreknowledge, seven ways He will deal with a sinful mankind. The first four ways have been exposed to us already in the Old Testament, whereupon there comes a juncture and the voice is heard of an eagle: "flying through the midst of heaven, saying with a loud voice: Woe, woe, woe to the inhabitants of the earth: by reason of the rest of the voices of the three angels who are yet to sound the trumpet" (8:13). The final three trumpets (and vials) deal (as a type) with the Church's awkward position in the hands of a reluctant Christianity.

"And in the sight of the throne was, as it were, a sea of glass like to crystal: and in the midst of the throne and round about the throne, were four living creatures, full of eyes before and behind" (4:6). God's infinite foreknowledge is crystal clear. His omniscience is as eyes in the midst of, and round about the throne. All existence is to Him an open book. "And I saw in the right hand of Him that sat on the throne, a book written within and without, sealed with seven seals. And I saw a strong angel, proclaiming with a loud voice: Who is worthy to open the book, and to loose the seals thereof? And no man was able, neither in heaven, nor on earth, nor under the earth, to open the book, nor to look on it. And I wept much, because no man was found worthy to open the book, nor to see it. And one of the ancients said to me: Weep not; behold the lion of the tribe of Judah, the root of David, hath prevailed to open the book, and to loose the seven seals thereof" (5:1-5).

It is the Lamb of God, Jesus Christ, Son of David, the conquering Messianic King, who is empowered because of his plenitude of power and his plenitude of wisdom, to break open the seals and read the enigma of the world's history. Each seal reveals the universe from heaven's point of view, what a new set of visions (the seven Trumpets and Vials) will show under different, or, rather, more concrete symbols. However, if a corner of the scroll were lifted just enough to arouse speculation of the Son of God becoming Man, as for example the breaking of the first seal reveals, then, for Lucifer, that would pose a problem. "And I saw: and behold a white horse, and he that sat on him had a bow, and there was a crown given him, and he went forth conquering that he might conquer" (6:2). This is Christ going forth to subdue the world by his Gospel. Any inkling of this would affect Lucifer strongly. Could he accept the mind-boggling proposition that the Word of God would become incarnate?

He was shielded, however, from knowing it clearly (as the knowledge of God), thus preventing an immediate revolt. This imagery of a conquering Christ on a white horse also fits the description of Lucifer opposing (being appalled by) whatever inkling he had of the "robbery" of God becoming Man. This would answer those who apply Apoc 6:2, exclusively to Christ on the white horse. And it would answer others who apply that passage to Lucifer, who, strangely enough, is the one perched on the white horse—protecting the "dignity" of God. Unknown to him, Lucifer's untested faithfulness, truth and justice were soon to be tested against the faithfulness, truth and justice of the Word of God become flesh. That is why it is only fitting that in the end, Christ would triumph on a white horse: "And I saw heaven opened, and behold a white horse; and he that sat upon him was called faithful and true, and with justice doth he judge and fight" (Apoc 19:11).

The opening of the seventh seal coincides with the moment of decision for Lucifer. "And when he had opened the seventh seal, there was silence in heaven, as it were for half an hour. And I saw seven angels standing in the presence of God; and there were given to them seven trumpets, And another angel came, and stood before the altar, having a golden censer; and there was given to him much incense that he should offer of the prayers of all saints upon the golden altar, which is before the throne of God. And the smoke of the incense of the prayers of the saints ascended up before God from the hand of the angel" (8:4). As mentioned, the scroll contains the foreknowledge of, among other things, the everlasting worship of God by all creation. But at the moment Adam was created, this foreknowledge, so to speak, arose like incense out of the golden censer; it began to ignite in the sight of God, and became activated.

To Lucifer, from his lofty height, lowly man, slime of the earth became an accomplished fact. His revulsion could no longer remain checked. The creation of man was enough to confirm his suspicions about the Son of...Man, a thought so repugnant to his concept of deity, that it led

to his downfall. "And the angel took the censer, and filled
it with the fire of the altar, and cast it on the earth, and
there were thunders and voices and lightnings, and a great
earthquake." Not without "thunders and voices and lightnings," did this prince of Light and his lesser lights become dislodged from their places before the throne of God.
Their very loss of tranquility of order reacted as "a great
earthquake," as they faced the prospect of being trumpeted
from their heavenly abode. "And the seven angels, who
had the seven trumpets, prepared themselves to sound the
trumpet" (Apoc 8:6).

XV

The Seven Wraths Of God

Trumpets symbolize the summons of God, especially to Judgment, but also the promulgation of feasts and disasters. (Apoc 16) becomes even more graphic in that the seven angels are given bowls containing the plagues in which is consummated the wrath of God. Be it observed, therefore, seven times shall the world be visited in an extraordinary way if a certain pattern of sin persists. Already we have seen Satan dislodged from heaven. "And the first angel sounded the trumpet, and there followed hail and fire, mingled with blood, and it was cast on the earth, and the third part of the earth was burnt up, and the third part of the trees was burnt up, and all green grass was burnt up" (8:7). Earth was not to be the same as it felt the hot breath of Satan, who, like a roaring lion began going about seeking someone to devour. Nothing would delight him more than to see all creation "groaning in travail."

But Apoc16 describes more graphically how this scourge from heaven is to be the potential sore spot of men and seducer of those who would permit themselves to become perverse: "And I heard a great voice out of the temple, saying to the seven angels: Go, and pour out the seven vials of the wrath of God upon the earth. And the first went, and poured out his vial upon the earth, and there fell a sore and grievous wound upon men, who had the character of the beast; and upon them that adored the image thereof" (16:1-2). Satan's cunning, if permitted to confront Adam would be more than adequate. His tempting of Adam however, would place him in direct confrontation with the Son of Man. Implicit in the fall of Adam (wounding) would be the seduction of mankind (character of the beast) away from their Savior. "The mystery of iniquity" would be quite inadequate against the "Mystery" of redemption, but Satan resolved his dilemma by employing the seductive powers of "Jezebel." This is confirmed by the pouring of the second vial, which corresponds to Adam's fall from grace, and loss of tranquility of order. "And the second angel poured out his vial upon the sea, and there came blood as it were of a dead man; and every living soul died in the sea" (16:3). The sea of posterity as it were turned red by Original Sin..."which kills by the death of one man, Adam."

The second angel with the trumpet reveals the effects of Original Sin in a less devastating light. Though "all died" in Adam, he, and they in him were spared the ultimate punishment of banishment from God. "And the second angel sounded the trumpet: and as it were a great mountain, burning with fire, was cast into the sea, and the third part of the sea became blood: And the third part of those creatures died, which had life in the sea, and the third part of the ships was destroyed" (8:8,9). When Adam the "great mountain" (of red earth) was cast into the sea, the damage was to be only a partial blindness (the third part of those creatures) and a partial loss of order and tranquility (the third part of the ships).

XVI

The Deluge

Some time after the fall of our first parents, God saw "that the wickedness of men was great on the earth, and that all the thought of their heart was bent upon evil at all times" (Gen 6:5). This time it was due to the intercession of Noe that He did not blot out man from the face of the earth, but He gives a signal for the angel with the third trumpet: "And the third angel sounded the trumpet, and a great star fell from heaven, burning as it were a torch, and it fell on the third part of the rivers, and upon the fountains of waters: And the name of the star is called Wormwood. And the third part of the waters became wormwood; and many died of the waters, because they were made bitter" (Apoc 8:10,11).

God found favor with the just man Noe, and thus His own Justice was prevailed upon to spare the world from extinction. But like a great star His Justice streaked from heaven, burning as it were a torch of His Truth. Its contact with the rivers and the fountains of waters made those rivers and fountains bitter to the unjust who drank of it. Only the unjust (along with brute beasts, which all the more emphasized the wrath of God) died in the waters (made bitter as it were by wormwood) of the deluge. "He destroyed all the substance that was upon the earth, from man even to beast, and the creeping things and fowls of the air; and they were destroyed from the earth. And Noe only remained and they that were with him in the ark" (Gen 7:23).

The pouring out of the third vial, corresponding to the third trumpet, reveals how the Justice of God is truly exonerated by the deluge. "And the third poured out his vial upon the rivers and the fountains of waters; and there was made blood. And I heard the angel of the waters saying: Thou are just, O Lord, who art, and who wast, the Holy One because thou hast judged these things: For they have shed the blood of saints and prophets, and thou hast given them blood to drink; for they are worthy" (16:4-6). In this passage we find a deeper significance of God's wrath abhorring sins against His saints (such as Cain against Abel) as being more directly against Himself. "The voice of thy brother's blood crieth to me from the earth" (Gen 4:10). Hence the symbolism of waters being turned to blood. "And I heard another, from the altar, saying: Yea, Lord God Almighty, true and just are Thy judgments" (16:7).

XVII

Tower Of Babel

Next we get a lesson of God's displeasure for the sin of overweening human pride and self-sufficiency. The story of the Tower of Babel may provide us more with a lesson than with complete factual information. Yet the sin that it advertises is to be punished severely and in a two-fold manner. For example, when the fourth vial is poured out, the sun scorches with great heat; but when the fourth trumpet is sounded, the sun is darkened: "And the fourth angel poured out his vial upon the sun, and it was given unto him to afflict men with heat and fire: And men were scorched with great heat, and they blasphemed the name of God, who hath power over these plagues, neither did they penance to give him glory" (16:8,9).

One facet of pride leads to blasphemy and final impenitence. The tower of arrogance and self-sufficiency becomes vulnerable to scorching heat, for it leaves its element by not being founded on the bedrock of humility. The other side of pride leads to blind obstinacy, disharmony and confusion: "And the fourth angel sounded the trumpet, and the third part of the sun was smitten, and the third part of the moon, and the third part of the stars, so that the third part of them was darkened, and the day did not shine for a third part of it, and the night in like manner" (8:12). So that although the eyes of the proud may be wide open, a sort of double exposure causes blindness. Pride bedazzles the eyes to the self-evident truths of the sun by day and obscures the mysterious truths of the moon and stars by night.

XVIII

WOE, WOE, WOE

At this juncture an eagle announces further potential disasters. Perhaps this is a maneuver to draw attention to the ominous nature of the remaining three woes: "And I beheld, and heard the voice of one eagle flying through the midst of heaven, saying with a loud voice: Woe, woe, woe to the inhabitants of the earth: by reason of the rest of the voices of the three angels who are yet to sound the trumpet" (8:13).

XIX

DIVINE ROBBERY

A star, like that which once settled over the crib of the Christ Child, that is to say, the divinity of Christ, was to dim symbolically, as the Son of Man hung on the cross. As he offered himself to the Father for the redemption of many, his human nature within the hypostatic union was "abandoned" by the divine. "My God, my God, why hast Thou forsaken me" (Matt 27:46)? (Not to say that the uninterrupted beatific vision in the highest faculty of the soul is incompatible with bodily, mental and even spiritual suffering: e.g., the uselessness of his passion for some souls).

Not only did the divinity of Christ dim symbolically, but "smoke from the (bottomless) pit arose" so that darkness settled over the physical world as well. "Now from the sixth hour there was darkness over the whole earth, until the ninth hour" (Matt 27:45). "And the fifth angel sounded the trumpet, and I saw a star fall from heaven upon the earth, and there was given to him the key of the bottomless pit. And he opened the bottomless pit: and the smoke of the pit arose, as the smoke of a great furnace; and the sun and the air were darkened with the smoke of the pit" (Apoc 9:1,2).

XX

SATAN VS. THE CHURCH

Jesus descended into Abraham's bosom, the hell of
the dead, to comfort them with the news that the gates of
heaven were soon to be opened. But this cruel death of
Christ likewise reverberated through Sheol, the bottomless pit of Hades. That Christ was condemned and put to
death by the sins of men was in a sense a victory for the
powers of darkness. Yet now there had to come over Satan
a glaring certainty that Christ was indeed the divine One
whom he refused to serve. He must have had a presenti-
ment that his fate was to be sealed this time for sure. Instead, an antagonist was being prepared against that fallen
angel. This new antagonist would be empowered through
the redemptive merits of Christ to crush Satan speedily.

So it happened that Christ himself opened the bottomless pit, which is to say, he gave the powers of darkness permission to oppose the mission of his Mystical Body,
the Church, so that his mission from his Father might be
completed through men: "And from the smoke of the pit
there came out locusts upon the earth. And power was
given to them, as the scorpions of the earth have power"
(9:3).

Once again Satan was freed to salve his pride, as he
prepared his strategy (mystery of iniquity) against the
Catholic Church. The locusts are a symbol of all world-
enduring onslaughts upon God's elect. Satan keeps stirring up wicked men who become the very instruments of
hell. Some commentators explain these locusts as heretics

who have denied the divinity of Jesus Christ, such as Theodotus, Praxeas, Noetus, Paul of Samosata, Sabellius, Arius, etc.

XXI

THE UNTOUCHABLES

Satan's power against all of mankind, especially Christians, was curbed considerably: "And it was commanded them that they should not hurt the grass of the earth, nor any green thing, nor any tree: but only the men who have not the sign of God on their foreheads. And it was given unto them that they should not kill them; but that they should torment them five months: and their torment was as the torment of a scorpion when he striketh a man" (Apoc 9:4,5).

A fountain of grace opened up for those docile enough to be inscribed in the Book of Life. Perhaps the "grass of the earth" corresponds to children as well as adults who though not sufficiently aware of the Gospel message, nevertheless, as "little children" lead good lives in cooperation with the saving grace of Christ's redemption. Also, unbaptized children taken by death would enter the state of natural bliss. Secondly, the locusts were commanded not to hurt "any green thing." This mark of salvation corresponds to the theological virtue of Hope. For, Hope is as the verdure of the spiritual life. The Church represents Hope by the color green. Hope does indeed "spring eternal." Hope has such a delicate relationship with the other two theological virtues of Faith and Charity, and is so attuned to God as to epitomize the health of our soul: "For we are saved by hope" (Rom 8:24). Hope is the vigilance of faith and the perseverance of charity.

Finally, a third category, the Church (nor any tree) is inoculated against the death stings of Satan. We know for a fact that the Catholic Church will survive the onslaughts of Hell although the branches separated from her will wither away. As for the materialistic, the corrupt and the godless, there is a hopelessness surrounding their long history (symbolized by 5 months) of violence, treachery and revolt that is in marked contrast to the "peace of Christ surpassing all understanding."

XXII

THE FATE OF WORLDLINGS

The plight of those who trust in folly will be dire, "in those days." The next few passages perhaps reveal (typically) the horrifying destructive (nuclear, etc.) capacity of a world gone incoherent: "And in those days men shall seek death, and shall not find it: and they shall desire to die, and death shall fly from them. And the shapes of locusts were like unto horses prepared unto battle: and on their heads were, as it were, crowns like gold: and their faces were as the faces of men. And they had hair as the hair of women; and their teeth were as lions: And they had breastplates as breastplates of iron, and the noise of their wings was as the noise of chariots and many horses running to battle. And they had tails like to scorpions, and there were stings in their tails; and their power was to hurt men five months" (Apoc 9:6-10).

This life of bitterness culminating into a threat of near global anarchy and travail is what it will take (as a merciful providential prod) to stir up their salvific response to the divine lights they have been suppressing. As the sixth trumpet next reveals, the ecumenical mitigations will ease the way for the most abject of these harassed victims of the angel Exterminans. "And they had over them a king, the angel of the bottomless pit; whose name in Hebrew is Abaddon, and in Greek Apollyon; and in Latin Exterminans" (9:11).

XXIII

Fifth Vial

The pouring of the fifth vial corresponding to the fifth trumpet, penetrates the heart of the matter with its customary biting brevity. The seat of the problem is materialism, or worldliness. For, unless it be checked by, and especially within the highly endowed Church, will the hearts of men be permitted to lapse into the darkness of idolatry to the degree of the above-mentioned tenuous global condition. God will allow many stings of the locusts, as an alternate punitive source of grace rousing up the faith and salvaging the Church's compromised gospel effort. But despite these woes, men do not seem to repent of their idolatries—their sinful worship of whatsoever they prefer to God. "And the fifth angel poured out his vial upon the seat of the beast; and his kingdom became dark, and they gnawed their tongues for pain: And they blasphemed the God of heaven, because of their pains and wounds, and did not penance for their works" (16:10,11).

XXIV

The Sixth Trumpet

The second beast's efforts go unchecked and atheistic Communism spreads its deceit through many lands. The signal is given to the four angels, "who are bound in the great river Euphrates," to flaunt this menacing power against the Church. Our Lady of Fatima so predicted many calamities of this nature, such as nations being devastated because of her unheeded warnings. These calamities are typally portrayed in the Book of Revelation as three plagues of "fire, smoke and brimstone" issuing directly from the mouths of horses (Communist belligerency). The providential use of Communism's world-wide havoc as an agency of conversion is the penalty Catholics are paying for today for having prevented the Church from directly bridging the mighty Euphrates (to Christian unity). By compromising the Church's last call for traditional church reform (as proposed by Our Lady at Fatima) Catholicism entered the Church's appointed time for Gospel fulfillment in desperate need of an alternative Providential assistance.

As will be pointed out later, the divine intervention whereby the peoples may cross over the (ecumenically dried up) bed of the Euphrates, leaves the Christian unification vulnerable to the inroads of Satan's Anti-Christ. And so, to repeat, through a sufficiently Christian effort the Church had the potential of bridging the Euphrates so that this great river would by its force keep mankind impregnable against the strategy of Satan's three plagues.

"And the sixth angel sounded the trumpet: and I heard a voice from the four horns of the golden altar, which is before the eyes of God, saying to the sixth angel who had the trumpet: Loose the four angels, who are bound in the great river Euphrates. And the four angels were loosed, who were prepared for an hour, and a day, and a month and a year: for to kill the third part of men. And the number of the army of horsemen was twenty thousand times ten thousand. And I heard the number of them. And thus I saw the horses in the vision: and they that sat on them, had breastplates of fire and of hyacinth and of brimstone, and the heads of the horses were as the heads of lions: and from their mouths proceeded fire, and smoke, and brimstone. And by these three plagues was slain the third part of men, by the fire and by the smoke and the brimstone, which issued out of their mouths. For the power of the horses is in their mouths and in their tails. For, their tails are like to serpents, and have heads: and with them they hurt.

And the rest of the men, who were not slain by these plagues, did not do penance from the works of their hands, that they should not adore devils, and idols of gold, and silver, and brass, and stone, and wood, which neither can see, nor hear, nor walk: Neither did they penance from their murders, nor from their sorceries, nor from their fornication, nor from their thefts" (Apoc 9:13-21).

The universal plagues or depth of world degradation, anxiety and despair is expressed symbolically as a "third part of men" being slain. Obviously such a proportion (of over a billion people slain) would be too enormous a victory for Satan to be divinely permitted.

At this point (continuing the typal application of St. John's vision of the Vials) St. John skips over the climactic moment of truth, interposing it in chapter 11. He is content to witness the reconciliation process itself. The millennium, a period of conversion and instruction and unification into the one true fold where peace reigns, is represented as an angel descending from heaven having a symbol of peace, a rainbow over his head: "And I saw another mighty angel come down from heaven, clothed with a cloud, and a rainbow was on his head and his face was as the sun, and his feet as pillars of fire. And he had in his hand a little book open: and he set his right foot upon the sea, and his left foot upon the earth" (10:1,2).

XXV

ECUMENICAL REGISTRAR

The little book in the angel's hand was opened (ecumenically) and readied to receive the names of all men into the unity of one faith in God under Christ's authorship. The miraculous conversion and subsequent period of instruction would commence by a signal to the Holy Spirit to come renew the face of the earth. It is a generous pouring forth of the seven Gifts of the Holy Spirit ("seven thunders") of Wisdom, Understanding, Knowledge, Counsel, Piety, Fortitude and Fear of the Lord that will renew the face of the earth: and only through a healthy fruition of the Holy Spirit's Charity, Joy, Peace, Patience, Benignity, Goodness, Longanimity, Mildness, Faith, Modesty, Continency, Chastity, (Gal 5:22), will men begin to be reconciled with one another in Christ.

He is "the spirit of adoption of sons, whereby we cry Abba, Father" (Rom 8:15). "And He cried with a loud voice as when a lion roareth. And when He had cried, seven thunders uttered their voices" (Apoc 10:3). The divinely watered flower of Hope shall bloom in glory. "Careful to keep the unity of the Spirit in the bond of peace. One body and one Spirit; as you are called in one hope of your calling. One Lord, one faith one baptism. One God and Father of all, who is above all, and through all and in us all" (Eph 4:3-6).

XXVI

CHINK IN THE CHURCH'S ARMOR

Ebullient with ecstasy and overwhelmed by the excitement of the moment, St. John thought he could write alleluia, it is accomplished, thanks be to God, amen! But an angel tempered his fervor. The evangelization was not completed, and the good tidings of Christ's final victory could not yet be declared. And unfortunately, the gratuity of the ecumenical dispensation aided by the seven thunderclaps left the Church's reception of those thunderclaps tenuous. The weaker among the converts, who would benefit most by this general amnesty would, by the same token retain their vulnerability to the seductions of Anti-Christ.

The words, "That time shall be no longer" refer to the readiness of Anti-Christ to gather his forces, at which point there shall be no delay: "And when the seven thunders had uttered their voices, I was about to write: and I heard a voice from heaven saying to me: Seal up the things which the seven thunders have spoken; and write them not. And the angel, whom I saw standing upon the sea, and the things which are therein: That time shall be no longer. But in the days of the voice of the seventh angel, when he shall begin to sound the trumpet, the mystery of God shall be finished, as he hath declared by his servants the prophets" (Apoc 10:4-7).

XXVII

APOSTASY

St. John's vision now focuses (typally) on those taking most advantage of the ecumenically conditioned Church. Their entrance into the little book wherein unity is signified (one Fold, one Shepherd) is aided by a divine push through the back door (loophole) of fear and tribulation, rather than through the Church's narrow gate of evangelical love and virtue. The fickleness of human nature would not change noticeably in many of these poor souls, even during the sanctuary of the millennium. Manna from heaven would not prevent them from daydreaming on occasion about the "fleshpots of Egypt." For them the spirit of unity would leave something to be desired.

This little book, therefore, when first eaten by St. John, would be sweet to the mouth but its contents showing this delightfully tasting unity to be vulnerable to wide scale apostasy, became bitter to the belly: "And I heard a voice from heaven again speaking to me, and saying: Go, and take the book that is open, from the hand of the angel who standeth upon the sea, and upon the earth. And I went to the angel, saying unto him, that he should give me the book. And he said to me: Take the book, and eat it up: and it shall make thy belly bitter, but in thy mouth it shall be sweet as honey. And I took the book from the hand of the angel, and ate it up: and it was in my mouth sweet as honey: and when I had eaten it, my belly was bitter. And he said to me: Thou must prophesy again to many nations, and peoples, and tongues, and kings" (Apoc 10:8-11).

XXVIII

MAGIC WAND

St. John's vision of the measuring of the Jewish temple lends itself (typally) as a "measuring" in the order of a dispensation to Catholicism. The Church's frequently abused liturgies, strict observances and inherent horror of sin are temporarily eased (measured) as if by an ecumenical magic wand, in order mercifully to compensate the hitherto unreached world's neglected gospel access into the City of God's promised completion in Christ. It is a divine intervention sadly reminiscent of the "bills of divorce" granted to the chosen people by Moses when it appeared they were headed for schism. "And there was given me a reed like unto a rod: and it was said to me: Arise, and measure the temple of God, and the altar and them that adore therein" (Apoc 11:1).

The temple is to be measured, but not the outer court. The court is the court of the Gentiles, or court of Sin, and is reserved for the chaining of Satan for "a time, times and half a time" (Dan 7:25). This mysterious expression of Daniel can perhaps be explained as three stages of the millennium that the new Jerusalem (the Church) will enjoy while Satan is chained. They are: the period of conversion (birth), school of indoctrination (growth), and fruition of union of all peoples with the Lamb of God. In this way the millennium (symbolically 42 months) will take the life of Christ as its model, corresponding to the "time" Jesus spent in Mary's womb; "the times" of his hidden life; and the "half a time" of his public life: 9+30+3=42.

What is of interest here is that the "time," understood symbolically as nine months, may be taken as the preliminary stage or gradual entrance over a period of many years leading almost imperceptibly into the millennium. "But the court, which is without the temple, cast out, and measure it not: because it is given unto the Gentiles, and the holy city they shall tread under foot two and forty months:" (Apoc 11:2). Satan is firmly secured in the court of Sin just outside the walls of the millennial sanctuary—but his presence is felt there (anticipated), as he blasphemes (tramples) all that is good and sacred.

XXIX

Two Witnesses

St. John's "measuring of the temple," in an accommodated sense corresponds to the Traditional Church's
providential mitigation of its gospel prerogative over Satan. In effect, Vatican II's ecumenical dispensation signified the Church's failure to snuff out Satan's "mystery of
iniquity." And this precisely is the situation our Lady of
Fatima warned would culminate into the worldwide
scourge of atheistic Communism plaguing the two sources
of the Church's efficacious gospel calling. In other words,
this godless scourge would bide the time of its initial weakness, using belligerency and seduction in an attempt to
maneuver against and "kill" the two witnesses of the
Church...which are Scripture and Tradition. They corre-
spond to St John's two witnesses of the Synagogue: Moses
and Elias.

This forcing of Scripture and Tradition into "sackcloth" and this "killing" would even manifest itself most
forcibly, for example, by certain liberal adaptations that
would restructure the Church along humanistic lines. "And
I will give unto my two witnesses, and they shall prophesy
a thousand two hundred sixty days, clothed in sackcloth.
These are the two olive trees, and two candlesticks, that
stand before the Lord of the earth. And if any man will
hurt them, fire shall come out of their mouths, and shall
devour their enemies. And if any man will hurt them, in
this manner must he be slain. These have power to shut

heaven, that it rain not in the days of their prophecy: and they have power over waters to turn them into blood, and to strike the earth with all plagues as often as they will" (Apoc 11:3-6).

Scripture is a "two-edged sword," and the Gospel is the power of God: "For I am not ashamed of the Gospel. For it is the power of God unto salvation to every one that believeth" (Rom. 1:16). Catholic tradition likewise is divinely inspired, for the Holy Spirit preserves values and truths passed on by word of mouth as well as through the written word. The centuries would produce many "antichrists" who would deny the Father and the Son, and dissolve Jesus...but Scripture and Tradition would dispose of them and not the other way around. "And every spirit that dissolveth Jesus, is not of God: and this is Antichrist, of whom you have heard that he cometh, and he is now already in the world" (1 John 4:3).

The strong-arm tactics of bending, twisting and warping Scripture, of ignoring and ridiculing the traditional wisdom of the science of the saints would wrest many concessions from the legitimate ecumenical inspiration. As for the other inimical antichrists, they will come out to rejoice that, "God is dead," and that the two witnesses (the olive trees and lamps which were to give oil and light to the City of God) were shriveled up and snuffed out: "And when they shall have finished their testimony, the beast, that ascendeth out of the abyss, shall make war against them, and shall overcome them, and kill them" (11:7). The effects of truth and traditional values will seem to be but cadavers on the streets of the great city Jerusalem. But take note. The dancing in the streets happens, not because the two witnesses are dead, for they are not dead, but only suppressed. Their suppression is what relieves the pain of the near-dead consciences of worldlings.

Little do they know that the Church's ecumenical stage is being set for a sudden rejuvenation of the Word of God, and a rediscovery of sacred tradition. "And their bodies shall lie in the streets of the great city, which is called spiritually, Sodom and Egypt, where their Lord also was crucified. And they of the tribes, and peoples, and tongues, and nations, shall see their bodies for three days and a half: and they shall rejoice over them, and make merry: and shall send gifts one to another, because these two prophets tormented them that dwelt upon the earth. And after three days and a half, the spirit of life from God entered into them. And they stood upon their feet, and great fear fell upon them that saw them. And they heard a great voice from heaven, saying to them: Come up hither. And they went up to heaven in a cloud: and their enemies saw them. And at that hour there was made a great earthquake, and the tenth part of the city fell: and there were slain in the earthquake, names of men seven thousand: and the rest were cast into a fear, and gave glory to God of heaven" (11:8-13).

XXX

The Sixth Vial

"And the sixth angel poured out his vial upon the great river Euphrates; and dried up the water thereof, that a way might be prepared for the kings from the rising of the sun" (16:12). The strategy of the Dragon working through the First and Second beasts could succeed only insofar as Christians should fail to maintain an acceptable degree of holiness. "But doing the truth in charity, we may in all things grow up in him who is the head, even Christ. From whom the whole body, being compacted and fitly joined together, by what every joint supplieth, according to the operation in the measure of every part, maketh increase of the body, unto the edifying of itself in charity" (Eph 4:15,16). And since this evil strategy included the infiltration of the Church itself, there could come a point where she could no longer completely depend on her traditional spiritual resiliency for the accomplishment of her mission to the world.

Yet, her mission, namely, the reconciliation of all men with one another in the completion of the One Fold under Christ, is destined to succeed. Rivers of grace were originally intended to flow through this Church founded by Christ on the rock, Peter, and eventually bridge all opposition to the truth. Accordingly, the great river Euphrates represents the obstacle to Catholicism's direct fulfillment of its mission of unity. The kings of the east represent the world to be harvested. But Catholicism's failing (all the more confirmed by the traditional Church's insufficient Fatima response) to bridge the Euphrates, the river then would have to be dried up. That is to say, traditional Church reform no longer commensurate to the world's unfulfilled spiritual capacity for conversion, would be providentially mitigated in order to aid the conversion process.

Since the final outcome of the Church's gospel mission over Satan was never at stake, the Apocalypse could never have had reference to the world's physical ending. The battle between Satan and the Church, therefore, was a moral contest over the manner in which the Church's assured final "millennial" victory would be secured: directly and unconditionally—or, and this is Satan's apocalyptic concession—indirectly by means of an added stimulus produced by Satan's diabolic plagues (persecutions), with a condition attached, namely, that the Church's conquest of these final Armageddon-like plagues of Satan be followed by a brief but cataclysmic incursion of Anti-Christ.

Catholicism's lost missionary prerogative over Satan came at a great price to the Church, for it involved an apocalyptic shift away from the traditional Church's intermediary prerogative for fulfilling her evangelical calling. For example, the very first soul-searching agony the ecumenically-minded Church had to endure was an alarming evaporation of priestly and religious vocations, which, until the opening of Vatican II had been uniquely inherent within the Church's evangelical calling. Ironically, the kings of the east having been unreached by Catholicism's gospel effort in their behalf, quickly proceeded to transform the world itself into a catalytic agent of fear and chaos. Our Lady at Fatima had appealed to the Church to exercise her traditional values for preventing the release of "the errors of Russia" upon the world. And, if we read between the lines we see that Mary was quick to point out the painful prospect of those errors being punitively utilized as a providential alternative for stimulating a harassed mankind inwardly and ultimately towards the Church unity which she characterized as Russia's conversion to her Immaculate Heart.

It was no wonder Catholicism's compromised Fatima test was patterned after the same messianic confrontation the Jews experienced following Christ's teachings, miracles, exhortations and apocalyptic threats. In short, one last generation of Jews was held accountable for the House of Israel's whole mosaic legacy of faith. And so, Christ earnestly beseeched his people, and frequently aided them in their decision-making by the miracles of "one greater than Moses" to accept him directly and unconditionally in accordance with the House of Israel's mosaic prerogative of faith. By his own words Christ opened to them an entrance into the New Jerusalem's direct and unconditional gospel mission of reconciliation in, through and by his infinite merits—even though those infinite merits be but the shedding of one drop of his blood in obedience to his Father's will.

The tragedy is that although Israel's final acceptance of her promised Messiah was assured her (either directly or indirectly) by virtue of God's covenant with Abraham, nevertheless her sin of apostasy threw her blindly at the feet of the gentiles (in true apocalyptic horror at the burning of The Temple) to whom God then turned as the newly chosen gospel intercessors for His Son's redemptive mission to mankind. So too the Fatima generation, unknowingly to itself, was made accountable for the whole traditional Church's 2000 years Catholic legacy at the appointed time of the Church's gospel calling—which is to say, "the hour, the day, the month and the year (Apoc 9:15), in salvation history. It is only fitting that the mother of our Savior and of his Church should have entered into that pivotal point of salvation history. It is only fitting for her who was so powerfully designated as the "woman clothed with the sun, and the moon under her feet, and on her head a crown of twelve stars" (Apoc 12:1).

How else do we explain that four good angels were released, who had been bound at the great river Euphrates and had been held ready for "the hour, the day, the month, and the year to kill a third of mankind"? (Apoc 9:14) It makes no sense to say that until an appointed time mentioned here, the angels were fettered from opening to Satan his anticipated floodgate of persecutions against the Church. Even the holy martyrs in heaven were beginning to ask how much longer must the Church be subjected to these continuous persecutions. On the contrary, if these angels were fettered it was because they had to await the outcome of Satan's "mystery of iniquity." It is in this context that the Church's guardian angels had been readying themselves for the providential outcome of Catholicism's intermediary day of reckoning. In other words, Catholicism's sufficiently meritorious gospel response would have kept sealed the (conditionally revealed) apocalyptic plagues of the sixth seal—which in turn automatically included yet another satanic release against the Church by the seventh seal's Anti-Christ.

XXXI

Three Frogs

In a double vision interposed, St. John revealed (typally) how the Dragon would penetrate the holy sanctuary of Christian utopia: by three large ugly frogs crossing the dried up Euphrates. The irony is that the very providential concession that dries up the Euphrates becomes the Achilles heel of the millennium. If the Church had completed her mission to the world directly (without the ecumenical concession), the river Euphrates would have been bridged so that all of mankind might enter her invulnerable gates. But because of the feeble spiritual condition of many of the non-proselytized masses, many of those forced to take advantage of the ecumenical concession not only would remain vulnerable to the powers of darkness, but they themselves would provide Satan access into their millennial utopia. This is symbolized by the mighty Euphrates, which was powerfully endowed to wash away Satan's three ugly nocturnal creatures (the power of the ten kings, Anti-Christ and apostasy). And so, the providential concession drying up the river, by the same token gives access to Satan's three infiltrating hopping frogs into the millennial utopia.

Alas, the Church, by bridging the Euphrates could have directly repulsed the frogs through three spirits of her own: Through humility, "Little ones, I address you, for through his Name your sins have been forgiven" (1 John 2:12); through fortitude, "I address you, young men, for you are strong and the word of God remains in you, and you have conquered the evil one" (Ibid 14); and through a persevering love of truth, "Fathers, I address you, for you have known him, who is from the beginning" (Ibid 13). Unfortunately the mystery of iniquity unfolds into the lap of Anti-Christ: "And I saw from the mouth of the dragon and from the mouth of the beast, and from the mouth of the false prophet, three unclean spirits like frogs. For they are the spirits of devils working signs, and they go forth unto the kings of the whole earth, to gather them to battle against the great day of the Almighty God" (Apoc 16:13,14).

XXXII

Divine Intervention

Christ will intervene for a moment to reassure the elect and the faithful, as well as the newly made converts who are beginning to walk in the ways of faith, while increasing in virtue, that they will not be disgraced. "Behold, I come as a thief. Blessed is he that watcheth, and keepeth his garments lest he walk naked, and they see his shame" (Apoc 16:15). Christ's coming to the children of the millennium as a thief to strengthen and console them surely indicates that the aforementioned presence among them (as the Lamb ruling them) will be an Eucharistic presence. They will be bolstered so as to endure the onslaughts of the Second Beast, Stalin.

In other words, the powers of Communism so to speak will be revitalized by the dragon. But alas, at the merciful sounding of the seventh trumpet, the harassing of the children of God will be finished, as they and the enemies of God await the Day of Judgment. "And the seventh angel sounded the trumpet: and there were great voices in heaven saying:

"The kingdom of this world is become
Our Lord's and His Christ's, and
He shall reign for ever
and ever,
Amen!"

(The Apocalypse, 11:15)

Appendix

A Few Aphorisms by the Author

Faith

Faith is God's point of view.

Faith makes believers out of us. "...the word of God, which effectually works also in you that believe" (1 Thess. 2:13).

Faith: Making I contact with God.

Mystery is the sweatshop of reason and the sweetshop of faith.

We find it hard to believe the Didymus found it so hard to believe.

Out of the lattices of human nature I cry to thee O Lord. Lord hear my prayer.

Prayer helps faith to congeal; faith helps prayer to flow.

Confidence is to prayer what instant is to coffee.

Confidence in God
A reverent beseech-
With a boardinghouse reach.

HOPE

Hope is the difference between a hang in and a hang up.

Hope is honesty in the know.

Hope has a subtle way of tipping the future.

Hope: light at the beginning of the tunnel.

Hope tugs at the Mercy of God.

Hope is never mathematically eliminated.

Our salvation is hope extract. "We are saved by hope" (Rom. 8: 24).

The faintest hope can preserve the virginity of trust.

Expectation is a self-inflicted promise.

Faith moves mountains; hope moves mountain climbers.

The ballot box is a kind of hope chest.

CHARITY

Love of God and love of neighbor: the golden paint brush and golden paint of perfection.

Never look down on another person. Always view him from above.

Love of self is the bow; love of neighbor is the string; love of God is the arrow.

Love of God knows no bounds. It knows only leaps and bounds.

God can be explained to everyone but a lover; He can be experienced by no one but a lover.

One does not make love to God. On the contrary, love makes oneself to God.

Love loves love.

If you must have a heart of stone - make it flint.

Give me a lever and I can move the world; give me a lover and I can move the heavens.

Three Schools of Thought
Saints and sinners are talking of love-
And the angels are smiling above.

MARY

Mary is a queen among angels and an angel among queens.

At the Annunciation the Angel Gabriel came as a prince and left as a page.

Mary is our compelling influence. She compels her Son to come to us, and us to come to Him.

To call Mary blessed helps fill the generation gap: "All generations shall call me blessed."

The Rosary is always said with feeling.

The Rosary is a cross in a bed of roses.

The Rosary by any other name would sound just as sweet.

> *Keepsake*
> In sorrowful years
>   Like welling tears.
> In joyful hours,
>   Like scented flowers.
> In glorious days,
>   Like lumious rays:
>   The Rosary.

LIFE

Life presents only golden opportunities. To do good is golden; to do evil is a golden opportunity missed; to repent is golden.

"Life" always has the big "if" in the middle of it.

Life is a pilgrimage beweeen a why and a because.

Life is a boxcanjar existence.

Life begins at forty - except that where there once was a fuzzy chin there is now a fuzzy head.

Life is a spectator sport.

I am a firm beleiver in reincarnation. In my former life I was a teenager.

Ther is no life in outer space. God could not make the same mistake twice.

Goals
To live out
your life-
and out-live
your wife.

Order Form

Postal orders:
De La Salle Institute
Apocalypse Book
P.O. Box 3720
Napa, California   94558

Please send *Apocalypse* to:

Name:_____

Address:_____

City:_____ State:_____

Zip:_____

Telephone: (____) _____

Book Price: $10.00 in U.S. dollars.

Shipping: $4.00 for the first book and $1.00 for each additional
book to cover shipping and handling within US,
Canada, and Mexico. International orders add $7.00
for the first book and $3.00 for each additional book.